what
to
have
for
dinner

what to have for dinner

MARTHA STEWART LIVING WOULD LIKE TO THANK ITS FOOD EDITOR, SUSAN SPUNGEN,
FOR HER INSPIRATIONAL IDEAS AND RECIPES, WHICH MAKE UP A LARGE PART OF THIS VOLUME.

Manufactured in the United States of America.
Library of Congress Catalog Number: 95-071907
ISBN: 0-8487-1482-2 (hardcover)
0-8487-1483-0 (paperback)

EDITORS: Susan Wyland, Melissa Morgan, Amy Schuler

DESIGN: Laura Harrigan, Art Director of Special Projects
MARTHA STEWART LIVING

contents

spring

summer

autumn

winter

introduction

It is a question at least as old as civilization: What are we going to have for dinner?

We share this ritual of dinner with people everywhere. After a busy day, who doesn't look forward to both the meal and the company? For centuries, we have looked at the evening dinner as a symbol of family warmth and solidarity.

Because dinner is such a daily need, we often take it for granted. According to statistics, most families have the same few menus over and over again, probably because they are the ones the cook is comfortable making.

I got the idea for "What to Have for Dinner" from a little, old-fashioned book of the same title I found years ago. The book contained good, utilitarian food, not especially inspired, but there was real variety and an attempt at balanced nutrition.

We adopted the thesis of that little book, and every issue of MARTHA STEWART LIVING has included a feature titled "What to Have for Dinner." Each one offers four recipes that constitute a lovely, healthy, simple menu. Every recipe uses fresh, seasonal ingredients in creative ways. Most important, each menu introduces us to a way of eating that is different from our everyday, repetitive habits.

This book collects the best of the magazine's recipes in one illustrated volume, with preparation schedules and serving tips. While the menus are meant to be simple enough for everyday use, they are certainly sophisticated enough to be served to company as well.

Dinner is too important to skip or to take for granted. It can and should be a time to enjoy the ones we love, a time to share the good things of life. I hope you make these meals and enjoy them for a long time to come.

Martha Stewart

spring

Perhaps the ancient Romans and Babylonians had the right idea: They celebrated the new year in March, not in the middle of the cold, dark winter. After al!, spring is the season of beginnings, when everything is fresh, and certain foods are at their peak.

Asparagus—whether sautéed and tossed with shallots and sesame seeds or mixed with onions, red bell pepper, and tender young peas—is a favorite spring vegetable. Lamb chops, another classic spring dish, are coated with seasoned bread crumbs and garnished with fresh mint leaves. This is also the right season for introducing lighter dishes, such as fish and seafood: Salmon, sprinkled with fresh herbs and baked in parchment, is complemented by saffron couscous and a colorful chopped vegetable salad. Shrimp is sautéed in garlic and olive oil, then served over a bed of orzo, requiring nothing more than some leafy green spinach as an accompaniment.

In some cold climates, rhubarb is viewed as the first sure sign of spring. For dessert, this tart fruit lends its flavor to a rhubarb raspberry crisp. And although they're available throughout the year, strawberries are at their best starting in May. Here they take a somewhat exotic turn, topped with spiced whipped cream and crispy baked wontons.

RIGHT: Feta can be very salty, so keep this in mind when seasoning the salad.
BELOW RIGHT: A creamy yellow ware bowl is a good match for the saffron couscous.

CHOPPED SALAD with FETA CHEESE

serves 4

The ingredients for this colorful salad can be prepared in advance and stored in separate containers, leaving only the arrangement for the last minute.

2 heads Bibb lettuce or 1 head Boston lettuce, shredded
2 large carrots, cut into matchstick-size pieces
1 yellow and 1 red pepper, cut into matchstick-size pieces
3 beets, cooked, peeled, and cut into matchstick-size pieces (optional)
1 cucumber, peeled, seeded, and coarsely chopped
1 ripe tomato, cut into ½-inch chunks
4 radishes, sliced paper thin
1 head radicchio, shredded
2 heads Belgian endive, sliced
¼ pound feta cheese, crumbled
1 tablespoon Dijon mustard
¼ cup red-wine vinegar
   Salt and freshly ground pepper
¾ cup extra-virgin olive oil
   Chopped flat-leaf parsley, for garnish
   Watercress or mâche leaves, for garnish

1. Scatter shredded lettuce on a serving platter. Arrange the vegetables, radicchio, endive, and cheese in separate rows on top of lettuce.
2. Whisk together mustard, vinegar, salt, and pepper. Slowly whisk in olive oil. Drizzle dressing over salad, sprinkle with parsley and watercress or mâche leaves, add more pepper, and serve.

SAFFRON COUSCOUS

serves 4

Couscous, widely used in North Africa, is a tiny, grainlike pasta made from semolina flour that cooks very quickly.

1½ cups couscous
1½ cups chicken stock, preferably homemade
    Large pinch of saffron
    Salt (optional)
2   tablespoons unsalted butter (optional)
½   cup currants
½   bunch scallions, chopped
½   cup oil-cured black olives, pitted and slivered
    Freshly ground pepper

1. Put couscous in a large bowl. In a small saucepan, bring stock and saffron to a boil. Add salt to taste, if needed.
2. Pour stock over couscous, stir once or twice, and cover bowl tightly with a plate or aluminum foil. Let steam 10 minutes, then fluff with a fork; add butter if desired. Add currants, scallions, olives, and pepper. Toss to mix well; serve immediately.

1

CHOPPED SALAD with FETA CHEESE

SAFFRON COUSCOUS

SALMON and LEEKS BAKED in PARCHMENT

RHUBARB RASPBERRY CRISP

PREPARATION SCHEDULE

1 Assemble and bake rhubarb raspberry crisp.
2 Arrange salad and prepare vinaigrette; set aside separately.
3 Assemble and bake salmon.
4 Prepare couscous.
5 Drizzle salad with vinaigrette; sprinkle with chopped herbs.

SALMON and LEEKS BAKED in PARCHMENT

serves 4

Baking parchment can be purchased at kitchen-supply stores and some butcher shops. Use any fresh herb you like with the fish.

- 4 sheets parchment paper
- 4 salmon fillets, 6 to 8 ounces each
- 1 bunch leeks, washed well and sliced thin
  Dry white wine
  Olive oil
  Salt and freshly ground pepper
- 1 bunch chervil or other fresh herb, chopped
  Melted butter

1. Heat oven to 350°. Fold a large sheet of parchment paper in half and cut out a heart shape about 3 inches larger than fish fillet. Place the fillet near the fold, and place a handful of leeks next to it. Drizzle the fish with the wine and olive oil, and sprinkle with the salt, pepper, and chervil.

2. Brush edges of parchment paper with melted butter, fold paper to enclose fish, and make small overlapping folds to seal the edges, starting at curve of heart. Be sure each fold overlaps the one before it so that there are no gaps. Brush the outside of the package with melted butter. Repeat with rest of fillets.

3. Put packages on a baking sheet and bake until paper is puffed and brown, about 10 to 15 minutes.

ABOVE: Baking the salmon fillets in parchment also steams them, allowing all the flavors in the pouch to blend.

Contemporary white china, Italian crystal, and an antique American jelly jar filled with narcissi at each place setting make this a very special meal.

RHUBARB RASPBERRY CRISP
serves 4

*Rhubarb is delicious paired with sweet
fruits such as raspberries—or strawberries or
peaches—to temper its tartness.*

1½ pounds rhubarb, cut into 1-inch
     pieces (about 4 cups)
⅔   cup granulated sugar
     Zest and juice of 1 orange
1   cup all-purpose flour
½   cup dark brown sugar
½   teaspoon cinnamon
8   tablespoons (1 stick) cold unsalted
     butter, cut into small pieces
½   cup rolled oats
¼   cup hazelnuts, skinned, toasted,
     and chopped (optional)
½   pint fresh raspberries

1. Heat oven to 350°. Combine rhubarb,
granulated sugar, and orange zest and juice
in a large bowl. Stir to combine.

2. In another bowl, combine flour, brown
sugar, and cinnamon. Rub butter into flour
mixture with your fingers until it is well incorporated and large crumbs form. Add
oats and nuts and combine.

3. Turn rhubarb into a 1½-quart baking
dish, scatter raspberries evenly over surface, and cover with crumb topping. Bake
until topping is brown and crisp and juices
are bubbling, about 45 minutes. Let cool
slightly before serving.

ABOVE: An English ironstone bowl
with a slightly raised rim is ideal for
catching the juices from a luscious
rhubarb raspberry crisp.

RIGHT: This crisp will look better in a
white French porcelain tart pan than in
a tin pie pan.

RIGHT: A Chinese technique called dry sautéing helps the asparagus to retain its flavor.

FAR RIGHT: Like most Chinese dishes, the stir-fried chicken is a perfect blend of protein and carbohydrates.

BELOW: The cucumber and radish salad is served in a celadon bowl with a crackle glaze.

2

CUCUMBER
and RADISH SALAD

STIR-FRIED CHICKEN
with NOODLES

SESAME ASPARAGUS

STRAWBERRIES with
CRISP WONTONS

PREPARATION SCHEDULE

1 Assemble all ingredients and utensils.

2 Make crisp wontons.

3 Cook noodles.

4 Prepare vegetables for chicken.

5 Make cucumber salad.

6 Make asparagus and keep warm.

7 Stir-fry chicken and vegetables; serve with noodles.

8 Whip cream and slice strawberries; assemble desserts.

CUCUMBER and RADISH SALAD

serves 4

This cool and crunchy salad complements any spicy dish.

- 2 cucumbers, peeled
- 6 radishes, finely julienned
- 1 scallion, thinly sliced
  Red-pepper flakes
- 4 teaspoons rice-wine vinegar
- 1 teaspoon sugar
  Salt
- 2 tablespoons coarsely chopped peanuts or cashews

1. Quarter cucumbers lengthwise; run a knife under seeds to remove. Slice cucumbers at an angle into ½-inch-thick pieces.
2. Toss with radishes, scallion, red-pepper flakes, vinegar, sugar, and salt. Chill until ready to serve.
3. Divide among four salad plates and garnish each salad with chopped nuts.

STIR-FRIED CHICKEN with NOODLES

serves 4

Once you've assembled all the ingredients, the actual preparation time for this dish is minimal.

- 3 tablespoons peanut oil
- 2 cloves garlic, peeled and smashed
  3-inch piece of fresh ginger, peeled and cut into long, thin strips
- 2 whole boneless chicken breasts (1½ pounds), cut into strips
- 12 shiitake or white mushrooms, stems removed
- 1 red pepper, julienned
- 4 scallions (greens only), cut into 3-inch lengths
- 1 cup chicken stock
- 4 tablespoons low-sodium soy sauce
- 2 teaspoons rice-wine vinegar
- 2 teaspoons cornstarch, mixed with 2 teaspoons cold water
- 1 pound somen, soba, linguine, or spaghetti noodles, cooked
- 1 cup bean sprouts, as garnish
- 1 small bunch cilantro, as garnish
  Black or white sesame seeds, as garnish

1. Heat 2 tablespoons oil in a wok or heavy skillet. Add garlic and half the ginger; cook slowly until brown. Discard garlic and ginger.
2. Brown the chicken in the wok. Add the mushrooms, remaining ginger, pepper strips, and scallions; cook until soft, 3 to 4 minutes.
3. Add the stock, soy sauce, vinegar, and cornstarch mixture. Bring to a boil and cook for 2 minutes. Transfer to a bowl and keep warm.
4. In the wok, heat 1 tablespoon oil. Add the noodles and a few spoonfuls of sauce and heat. Top with the chicken mixture; garnish and serve.

SESAME ASPARAGUS

serves 4

This recipe uses a lower-fat version of a Chinese cooking technique called dry sautéing. The asparagus may also be served at room temperature.

- 1 pound fresh asparagus
- 2 tablespoons peanut oil
- 2 tablespoons minced shallots
- 1 tablespoon sesame seeds
- 2 teaspoons soy sauce (low sodium, if desired)
  Dash of dark sesame oil
  Freshly ground pepper

1. Trim the tough ends from the asparagus spears. Set spears aside.
2. Heat a 10-inch cast-iron skillet for about 2 minutes over medium-high heat. Add 1 tablespoon peanut oil and half of the asparagus in a single layer.
3. Cook for 3 to 4 minutes without turning. Shake pan occasionally. Turn and cook 3 minutes more. Asparagus should be bright green with brown spots.
4. Add 1 tablespoon shallots and half of the sesame seeds and c‑‑‑‑‑ ‑‑‑ ‑‑ pan to toss the asparagu‑ ‑‑‑ utes or until shallots ar‑ ‑‑‑‑ not let them burn.
5. Add half the soy sauc‑ ‑‑‑ pepper and cook for 30 s‑‑‑‑ to a plate and keep warm‑ ‑‑‑ remaining asparagus. K‑‑‑ ready to serve.

STRAWBERRIE‑ ‑‑ CRISP WONT‑‑

serves 4

Chinese five-spice pow‑‑ both sweet and savory dishe‑ hint of spice to the whi‑

- 4 wonton wrappers (s‑
- 1 tablespoon unsalted ‑
- 2 tablespoons plus 1 teaspo‑
- 2 pints fresh strawberries, hulled
- 1 pint heavy cream
  Pinch of five-spice powder or cinnamon and ground cloves

1. Heat oven to 425°. Brush both sides of wonton wrappers lightly with melted butter. Spread 2 tablespoons sugar on a plate and press skins into sugar to coat evenly on both sides. Place on a nonstick or buttered baking sheet. Bake for 4 to 5 minutes, or until wontons begin to turn golden brown. Turn and cook an additional 2 minutes or until evenly browned. Remove from baking sheet and let cool.
2. Slice the strawberries and toss with 1 teaspoon sugar. Whip the cream with five-spice powder or cinnamon and cloves.
3. Divide strawberries among four plates. Top with cream and a crisp wonton; serve.

NOTE: *Wonton skins are available in the produce or freezer section of most supermarkets as well as in Asian food markets. Unused wonton skins can be frozen for future use.*

OPPOSITE AND THIS PAGE: Low beige bowls, wooden chopsticks, an antique soy-sauce dish, traditional Chinese iron teapots, and celadon teacups are the perfect utensils for serving this Asian-inspired meal.

RIGHT: If you use fresh horseradish, grate it just before before adding to the sauce. This keeps the horseradish tangy.

3

CODFISH CAKES

HORSERADISH TARTAR SAUCE

BROCCOLI RABE, CARROT, and RADICCHIO SALAD

MANGO with WARM PINEAPPLE GINGER SAUCE

PREPARATION SCHEDULE

1 Make tartar sauce and assemble fish cakes.
2 Blanch broccoli rabe.
3 Whisk together vinaigrette.
4 Slice mangoes and make pineapple sauce.
5 Cook fish cakes.
6 Toss salad with vinaigrette.
7 Serve fish cakes with tartar sauce and salad.

CODFISH CAKES

serves 4

A food processor makes easy work of fish cakes, although they can also be made by hand.

3 tablespoons olive oil
1 large onion, finely chopped (about 1½ cups)
1½ teaspoons salt
¼ teaspoon freshly ground pepper
1¼ pounds cod or scrod fillets, bones removed
2 tablespoons finely chopped fresh tarragon leaves
1 egg, lightly beaten
3 dashes Tabasco, or to taste
⅓ cup dry bread crumbs

1. Heat oven to 200°. Heat 1 tablespoon olive oil in a skillet over medium heat. Add onion, ½ teaspoon salt, and ⅛ teaspoon pepper. Cook until onions are translucent, about 5 minutes. Set aside.
2. Cut fish into large chunks; pulse in a food processor to coarsely chop. Transfer to a medium bowl. Add onion, tarragon, egg, and Tabasco and combine well. Add remaining salt and pepper. Form eight 3-inch patties; dredge them in bread crumbs, shaking off excess.
3. Heat 1 tablespoon oil in a large skillet over medium-low heat. Cook 4 patties until browned, about 4 to 5 minutes on each side. Remove to a baking sheet, cover with aluminum foil, and keep warm in oven. Wipe out skillet, return to heat, and add remaining olive oil. Cook remaining patties and serve immediately with tartar sauce.

HORSERADISH TARTAR SAUCE

serves 4

Increase the horseradish to suit your taste.

1 stalk celery, finely chopped
2 tablespoons finely chopped cornichons or sour pickles
1 tablespoon prepared horseradish
2 tablespoons coarsely chopped flat-leaf parsley
½ teaspoon dry mustard
6 tablespoons mayonnaise
1 teaspoon lemon juice
   Salt and freshly ground pepper

In a small bowl, combine celery, cornichons, horseradish, parsley, mustard, mayonnaise, and lemon juice. Season to taste with salt and pepper and serve with the codfish cakes.

The bright colors of the broccoli rabe, carrot, and radicchio salad are the perfect foil for a plain white table setting.

The crunchy mix of vegetables in this
salad make it an excellent source of
vitamins A and C.

BROCCOLI RABE, CARROT, and RADICCHIO SALAD

serves 4

The sweetness of the carrots and honey is a good contrast to the bitterness of the broccoli rabe and radicchio.

1 tablespoon plus ½ teaspoon salt
1½ pounds broccoli rabe, tough stems removed and cut into 4-inch lengths
1 teaspoon lemon juice
1 teaspoon sherry vinegar
½ teaspoon honey
1 teaspoon low-sodium soy sauce
1 tablespoon olive oil
⅛ teaspoon freshly ground black pepper
4 small carrots, sliced into thin strips using a vegetable peeler
¼ head of radicchio, thinly sliced crosswise (1¼ cups)

1. Bring 3½ quarts cold water to a boil in a large pot and add 1 tablespoon salt. Add broccoli rabe and cook until just tender, about 1½ minutes. Drain and place in a bowl of ice water to stop the cooking process. Drain again and place on paper towels to absorb remaining water.
2. In a small bowl whisk together the lemon juice, vinegar, honey, soy sauce, and olive oil. Season with pepper and the ½ aspoon salt.
Combine broccoli rabe, carrots, and hio in a medium bowl. Drizzle the e over the vegetables, toss well to erve immediately.

MANGO with WARM PINEAPPLE GINGER SAUCE

serves 4

Buy the mangoes a day or two ahead of time to allow them to ripen.

1 fresh pineapple
1 vanilla bean, split in half
2 tablespoons sugar
1 teaspoon freshly grated ginger
2 mangoes
1 tablespoon crystallized ginger, roughly chopped

1. Remove the pineapple's top and skin. Cut pineapple lengthwise into quarters; remove core. Chop three quarters into large chunks; process in a food processor until smooth. Strain into a small saucepan.
2. Add vanilla bean, sugar, and fresh ginger to the pan and cook over medium heat, stirring often, until slightly thickened, about 8 minutes.
3. Meanwhile, dice the remaining quarter of the pineapple and place in a small bowl. Cut mangoes in half lengthwise, angling the knife slightly to cut around the elongated pit. Cut out and discard the pit. Peel mangoes and discard the peel. Cut the mangoes into bite-size pieces and divide among 4 plates.
4. Remove pineapple sauce from heat. Scrape the seeds from the vanilla bean, stir the seeds into the sauce, and discard the pod. Combine the warm sauce with the diced pineapple and spoon the sauce over each plate of sliced mango. Sprinkle with crystallized ginger and serve.

ABOVE: An unusual yellow-rimmed Leeds-ware plate reflects the colors of the mango, pineapple, and ginger.

4

MINTED PEA SOUP

STEAMED SPINACH

SHRIMP SAUTÉ
with ORZO

ALMOND BRITTLE SUNDAE

PREPARATION SCHEDULE

1 Make almond brittle.

2 Start soup; peel and
clean shrimp.

3 Wash spinach.

4 Puree and season soup;
start orzo; make croutons.

5 Cook shrimp; steam spinach.

A metal steamer is one of the best ways to cook vegetables so they retain color, flavor, and nutrients.

MINTED PEA SOUP

serves 4

This light, fresh-tasting soup is also delicious served chilled.

2 teaspoons olive oil
4 shallots, sliced
½ pound waxy potatoes, peeled and cut into 1-inch pieces
2 cups chicken stock, preferably homemade
1 10-ounce package frozen peas
6 ounces snow peas, trimmed and cut in half crosswise
½ cup fresh mint leaves, loosely packed
Salt and freshly ground pepper
2 slices white bread, cut into ½-inch cubes and toasted until golden brown, for croutons
¼ cup pea shoots (optional)

1. In a medium saucepan, heat oil over medium heat. Add shallots and sauté for 2 minutes. Add potatoes and chicken stock and bring to a boil, then reduce heat and simmer for 15 minutes, or until the potatoes are tender. Add frozen peas and snow peas and simmer for 3 more minutes, or until just tender and still bright green. Stir in mint leaves.

2. Remove pan from heat and allow to cool slightly. Puree the vegetables in small batches in a blender or food processor until smooth. Return to saucepan and heat through. Season with salt and pepper, ladle into bowls, and sprinkle with the croutons and pea shoots if desired.

STEAMED SPINACH

serves 4

The best way to rid spinach of grit is to immerse it in a sinkful of cold water, let sand settle on the bottom, and lift out spinach. Drain sink and repeat until no sand remains.

1 pound spinach, about 2 bunches
Juice of ½ lemon
Salt and freshly ground pepper
1 teaspoon unsalted butter (optional)

1. Wash spinach in several changes of cold water until free of sand. Remove stems.
2. Place a metal steamer in a medium saucepan filled with 1 inch of water. Bring to a boil. Add spinach, cover, and steam for about 3 minutes, or until just wilted. Remove from steamer and season with the lemon juice, salt, and pepper. Toss with butter if desired.

These utilitarian white porcelain bowls contrast vividly with the minted pea soup. The cream-colored napkin is linen and the spoon is antique silver.

Shrimp, one of the most popular shellfish, come in four sizes: tiny, medium, large, and jumbo (also called "prawns"). Most recipes call for the larger sizes, but tiny shrimp, usually sold in cans and frozen in bags, are often used when a shrimp flavor is called for. On average there are forty to forty-five tiny shrimp per pound and thirty to thirty-five medium shrimp. Large shrimp will yield twenty to twenty-five per pound, while the more expensive jumbo shrimp will yield ten to twelve. Although shrimp is caught on both the East and West coasts, more than half of the shrimp consumed in America is imported from countries like Ecuador and Thailand.

Unlike other seafood, most shrimp has already been frozen by the time you buy it, which does not affect its taste. It should not, however, be refrozen once defrosted, nor should it smell of chlorine or ammonia. Methods of peeling depend on the size of the shrimp. For tiny shrimp, simply discard the heads and remove the shell with your fingers. For medium, large, and jumbo shrimp, pull the head from the body, leaving the tail meat intact. Remove the legs and peel off the shell with your fingers, then make a shallow cut along the back and remove the dark intestinal vein.

SHRIMP SAUTÉ with ORZO

serves 4

Orzo is a rice-shaped pasta widely available in supermarkets.

1 cup uncooked orzo
1 tablespoon plus 1 teaspoon olive oil
  Salt and freshly ground pepper
2 cloves garlic, peeled and minced
20 large shrimp, peeled and deveined, tails left on
¼ cup finely chopped Italian parsley
  Juice and zest of 1 lemon
1 cup dry white wine
5 tablespoons unsalted butter
1 tablespoon capers, rinsed

1. Bring a medium saucepan of salted water to a boil. Add orzo; cook until al dente, using cooking time suggested on package. Drain, toss with 1 teaspoon oil, and add salt and pepper to taste.

2. Meanwhile, heat remaining oil in a large skillet. Add garlic; cook over low heat for 1 minute. Add shrimp, salt and pepper to taste, and 2 tablespoons parsley; cook for 3 to 4 minutes. Turn and cook for 3 minutes more, or until opaque. Remove from pan and keep warm.

3. Add lemon juice and wine to skillet. Bring to a boil, lower heat, and reduce by half, about 2 minutes. Remove from heat. Add remaining parsley; stir in butter, lemon zest, and capers. Adjust seasonings. Pour over shrimp, and serve on a bed of orzo.

ALMOND BRITTLE SUNDAE

serves 4

A little amaretto drizzled over the top makes this a sundae for grown-ups.

1 teaspoon vegetable oil, for baking sheet
¾ cup sugar
2 tablespoons water
½ cup sliced blanched almonds
1 pint vanilla frozen yogurt or ice cream
4 teaspoons amaretto (optional)

1. Oil a 9-by-13-inch baking sheet and set aside. Combine sugar and water in a heavy-bottomed saucepan. Cook over low heat until sugar is dissolved. Cover pan and bring to a boil. Leave cover on until condensation washes down insides of pan. Turn heat to medium and cook, swirling pan occasionally, until sugar turns amber in color and registers 320° on a candy thermometer. Quickly stir in almonds; pour mixture onto prepared baking sheet. Spread with back of a metal spoon until thin. Allow to cool completely; break into pieces, reserving some larger ones for garnish.

2. Scoop frozen yogurt or ice cream into wine or dessert glasses. Sprinkle with brittle and garnish with a large shard. Drizzle amaretto over top if desired.

Affordable hotel silver—pictured with the shrimp and orzo—is becoming increasingly popular with collectors.

Almond brittle turns plain vanilla frozen yogurt into a fancy dessert. Serve it in a vintage cocktail glass for an elegant touch.

SPRING CHICKEN RAGOUT

serves 4

*Stewing the chicken on the bone
makes it tender and juicy.*

2 whole chicken breasts (1¾ pounds),
   bone in, split and skinned
   Salt and freshly ground pepper
2 teaspoons olive oil
1¾ cups homemade or low-sodium
   canned chicken stock
4 canned plum tomatoes, seeded
   and quartered
12 baby carrots, peeled and trimmed
½ pound asparagus, trimmed and
   cut into 1½-inch pieces
1 leek (about 6 ounces), well cleaned
   and cut into ¼-inch rounds
1 cup shelled peas, preferably fresh
   Flat-leaf parsley, for garnish
   (optional)

1. Season chicken breasts with salt and
pepper. Heat olive oil in a large skillet, add
chicken, and cook over medium-high heat
until golden brown on both sides, about 7
minutes total.
2. Add stock and tomatoes, bring to a
boil, and cover. Cook on medium-low heat
for about 20 minutes, then remove the
chicken and set aside.
3. Add carrots to skillet and cook, covered, until almost tender, about 5 minutes.
Add asparagus, leeks, and peas and cook
until all the vegetables are tender, about 5
more minutes.
4. Meanwhile, pull chicken from bone
and shred into large bite-size pieces. Return chicken to the skillet and cook until
heated through, about 2 minutes. Serve
over the egg noodles and garnish with
sprigs of parsley, if desired.

EGG NOODLES with LEMON and HERBS

serves 4

*These old-fashioned egg noodles
are the perfect accompaniment to the
Spring Chicken Ragout.*

1 tablespoon plus ¾ teaspoon salt
8 ounces wide egg noodles
2 tablespoons butter, at room
   temperature
2 tablespoons coarsely chopped
   flat-leaf parsley
2 tablespoons snipped chives
   (about ½ bunch)
1½ teaspoons grated lemon zest
⅛ teaspoon freshly ground pepper

1. Fill a large saucepan with cold water,
bring to a boil, and add 1 tablespoon salt.
Add noodles and cook until tender but still
firm, about 5 minutes. Remove from heat,
drain noodles, and transfer to a bowl.
2. Add butter, parsley, chives, lemon zest,
remaining ¾ teaspoon salt, and pepper.
Toss to coat noodles with butter and
herbs. Serve immediately or keep warm,
covered with foil, until ready to serve.

A lemon zester—available in most
housewares stores—will make it easier
to flavor the egg noodles.

5

ARTICHOKES with OLIVES
and PARMESAN

EGG NOODLES with
LEMON and HERBS

SPRING CHICKEN RAGOUT

STRAWBERRY CRUSH

PREPARATION SCHEDULE

1 Freeze strawberries.

2 Trim and cook artichokes.
   Make dressing.

3 Prepare and cook ragout.

4 Cook noodles and toss
   with herbs.

5 Serve dinner.

6 Make and serve dessert.

Fresh spring vegetables can lighten a classic winter ragout: Spears of asparagus and sweet green peas have been added to the chicken. A wide-rimmed soup plate and a liner make for a more formal presentation.

Once the leaves on an artichoke start to open, it's past its prime, so look for ones with tight, overlapping leaves. Here, they're served in a flat-bottomed ironstone bowl.

ARTICHOKES with OLIVES and PARMESAN

serves 4

Choose artichokes that seem heavy for their size; they will have the largest hearts.

- 4 large globe artichokes (about 1 pound each)
- 3 lemons
- 4 teaspoons salt
- ½ cup extra-virgin olive oil
- 1 teaspoon sherry vinegar
- ½ teaspoon Dijon mustard
- ⅛ teaspoon freshly ground pepper
- 2 tablespoons finely chopped shallots (about 2 small)
- ¼ cup oil-cured olives, pitted and finely chopped
- ¼ cup freshly grated Parmesan

1. Trim 1 inch from artichoke stems and a quarter inch from tops. Remove tough outer leaves. Using scissors, cut sharp tips off leaves. Fill a large saucepan with 5 quarts cold water. Squeeze the juice of 2 lemons into water and add lemon halves to saucepan. Add artichokes, 3 teaspoons salt, and 2 tablespoons olive oil. Place a smaller lid on top to keep artichokes submerged and bring to a boil. Gently boil over medium-high heat until artichokes are tender when pierced in the heart with a paring knife, 25 to 30 minutes. Drain and let cool.

2. In a small bowl, combine juice from remaining lemon (2 to 3 tablespoons), vinegar, mustard, remaining salt, and pepper. Whisk in remaining olive oil, shallots, olives, and 2 tablespoons Parmesan.

3. Cut the stems of the artichokes flush to the base and serve on the side, if desired. Spoon the dressing evenly over the artichokes. Sprinkle with remaining Parmesan and serve.

STRAWBERRY CRUSH

serves 4

Raspberries, blackberries, or even peaches or bananas will work in this cool, fruity dessert.

- 4 cups strawberries, hulled and cut in half
- 1 cup ice cubes
- ¼ cup whole unblanched almonds
- ¼ cup sugar
- 3 tablespoons milk
- 2 tablespoons almond-flavored liqueur, such as Amaretto
- 2 teaspoons slivered unblanched almonds for garnish

1. Place strawberries in an airtight container or plastic bag and leave in the freezer for 1½ hours.

2. Remove strawberries from freezer. Place half of the frozen strawberries in the jar of a blender. Add ice, whole almonds, sugar, milk, and liqueur and as many more strawberries as will fit. Blend until there is enough room to add more strawberries. Add remaining strawberries and blend until smooth and spoonable. Divide among 4 serving dishes. Garnish with slivered almonds and serve immediately.

The strawberry crush can be poured straight from the blender into clear coupe glasses.

Seasonal vegetables like asparagus and fresh peas can be combined with year-round staples such as onion and red pepper for a simple sauté.

SAUTÉED SPRING PEAS, ASPARAGUS, RED PEPPERS, and ONIONS

serves 4

*You can also use frozen peas—
they only need defrosting.*

¾ pound fresh peas

¾ pound asparagus, cut obliquely into
   1-inch pieces

1 tablespoon olive oil

1½ teaspoons unsalted butter

1 small red onion, sliced into
   ⅛-inch rounds

1 large red bell pepper, seeded and
   cut into ⅛-inch strips

¾ teaspoon salt

¼ teaspoon freshly ground pepper

½ cup chicken stock, preferably
   homemade or low-sodium canned

1. Bring a large pot of salted water to the boil. Separately boil the fresh peas and asparagus until crisp-tender, about 1 minute. Plunge into cold water to stop the cooking process, and drain.

2. In a large skillet, heat olive oil and butter over medium heat. Add onion and bell pepper and cook until slightly wilted, about 3 minutes. Add peas, asparagus, salt, and pepper, and cook for 1 to 2 minutes. Increase heat to high and add chicken stock; cook until reduced by half, about 3 minutes. Serve immediately with lamb chops.

PARMESAN HERB CRUSTED LAMB CHOPS

serves 4

*Finishing the lamb chops in the oven
prevents the crumb crust from burning.*

¼ cup finely chopped flat-leaf parsley

¼ cup finely chopped fresh mint

½ cup fresh bread crumbs

½ cup freshly grated Parmesan

8 rib lamb chops (1½ pounds),
   chine bone removed

½ teaspoon salt
   Pinch of freshly ground pepper

2 large eggs, beaten

3 tablespoons olive oil

4 sprigs of mint, for garnish

1. Heat oven to 450°. In a medium dish, combine the parsley and mint and set aside. In another medium dish, combine the bread crumbs and cheese.

2. Sprinkle lamb chops with salt and pepper and press mint and parsley onto the chops, covering both sides. Dip chops into the beaten egg and then into the bread-crumb mixture, coating them well.

3. In a large nonstick skillet with a heat-resistant handle, heat olive oil over medium-high heat. Add chops and cook until well browned, about 2 minutes on each side. Carefully turn chops and brown the edges, about 30 seconds. Transfer skillet to the oven and finish cooking chops until medium rare, about 2 minutes. Serve immediately with sautéed spring peas, asparagus, red peppers, and onions.

The simplicity of white porcelain and unadorned linens lets the textures and colors of the herb-crusted lamb chops and sautéed vegetables come through.

Romaine doesn't get soggy as quickly as many other varieties of lettuces, so you don't have to wait until the very last minute to dress the salad with the tomato vinaigrette. The deep well of this octagonal dish makes it a nice alternative to a bowl.

HEARTS of ROMAINE with TOMATO VINAIGRETTE

serves 4

Save the outer leaves of the romaine for use in a salad the next day.

2   large heads romaine, about 1¼ pounds each
1½ cups (8 ounces) red cherry tomatoes, cut into quarters lengthwise
½   teaspoon salt
¼   teaspoon freshly ground pepper
½   teaspoon honey mustard
2   tablespoons champagne vinegar
3   tablespoons olive oil
1½ teaspoons coarsely chopped fresh marjoram

1. Remove the large outer leaves of the romaine down to the heart. Cut the hearts lengthwise into quarters, and divide them among 4 salad plates. Set plates aside in the refrigerator.
2. Place half the tomatoes in a food processor or a food mill and puree until smooth. Pass the puree through a strainer and discard solids. Set tomato puree aside.
3. In a medium bowl, whisk together salt, pepper, mustard, and vinegar. Whisking constantly, add olive oil in a slow, steady stream, until the dressing is amalgamated. Whisk in reserved tomato puree and the marjoram and stir in remaining quartered tomatoes. Pour dressing over hearts of romaine and serve immediately.

GIANT ALMOND CRUMB COOKIE

serves 4

Place this giant cookie in the center of the table and let guests break off chunks.

1½ cups (5¼ ounces) finely ground blanched almonds
1¾ cups all-purpose flour
¾   cup sugar
¼   teaspoon salt
1½ teaspoons vanilla extract
1¾ sticks unsalted butter, at room temperature
2   pounds red and/or green grapes, as an accompaniment

1. Heat oven to 350°. Butter a ten-inch springform pan and set aside. In a large bowl, whisk together all of the ingredients except for the butter and the grapes.
2. Cut in the butter with a pastry cutter or a fork until the mixture is crumbly. Continue working in the butter until it is completely incorporated and there are no dry crumbs. Squeeze the mixture together to create pea-size to 1-inch clumps.
3. Transfer three-quarters of the mixture to prepared pan. Gently press mixture into the pan to slightly compress the dough. Sprinkle remaining mixture over the top and transfer to oven. Bake until cookie begins to turn golden, about 25 minutes. Lower heat to 300° and bake until golden brown and fairly dry, about 10 more minutes.
4. Remove cookie from the oven and place on a wire rack to cool completely. Serve with chilled red and green grapes. This cookie keeps for 4 to 5 days when tightly sealed in aluminum foil.

This giant almond crumb cookie was inspired by one found in Ferrara, a small city in northern Italy. Silver grape shears and a crystal bowl of red and green grapes help make a homey dessert elegant.

7

SPICY TOMATO SOUP

PAPAYA, JICAMA,
and AVOCADO SALAD

TURKEY and
GREEN CHILE BURRITOS

COFFEE CUSTARD

PREPARATION SCHEDULE

1 Prepare and bake custard.

2 Make soup and let simmer.

3 Prepare filling for burritos.

4 Whisk together vinaigrette;
   make salad.

5 Roll and bake burritos.
   Cool custard.

6 Serve soup while burritos bake.

ABOVE: The large bowl of a cream-soup spoon is useful for scooping up the chunky tomato soup.

ABOVE RIGHT: The turkey and green chile burritos feature roasted poblanos, one of the milder chile peppers.

RIGHT: Papaya, jicama, and avocado make an unusual salad. Jicama, a root vegetable from Mexico, is available in many supermarkets. Don't buy avocados that are rock hard, since this means they were picked too early.

SPICY TOMATO SOUP

serves 4

*Cilantro stems are the secret to
this fresh-tasting soup.*

1   tablespoon olive oil
1   medium red onion (about 8 ounces),
    chopped into ½-inch dice
1   medium clove garlic, minced
1   teaspoon salt
⅛   teaspoon freshly ground pepper
¼   cup cilantro stems, cut into ½-inch
    lengths
½   jalapeño pepper, seeded and
    finely diced
1   28-ounce can plum tomatoes
1   tablespoon fresh lime juice
¼   cup sour cream

1. Heat olive oil in a deep saucepan over medium-low heat. Add onions and garlic and cook until onions are soft and translucent, about 5 to 7 minutes. Add salt, pepper, cilantro stems, and jalapeño.

2. Strain tomatoes and add the juice to the saucepan. Seed tomatoes, chop coarsely, and add to saucepan. Add 2 cups water and stir to combine. Simmer for about 30 minutes. Add the lime juice and adjust seasoning with salt and pepper. Divide among 4 soup bowls and serve with a dollop of sour cream.

PAPAYA, JICAMA, and AVOCADO SALAD

serves 4

This chunky and crunchy salad is served more as a condiment than a separate course.

¼ cup fresh lime juice
2 tablespoons olive oil
1 teaspoon salt
⅛ teaspoon freshly ground pepper
1 ripe papaya (about 1½ pounds), peeled, seeded, and cut into ½-inch dice
1 jicama (about 1 pound), skinned and cut into ½-inch dice
1 Haas avocado (about 12 ounces), ripe but firm
¼ cup cilantro leaves, coarsely chopped

1. In a small bowl, whisk together lime juice, olive oil, salt, and pepper; set aside.
2. In a medium bowl, combine the papaya and jicama. Cut avocado in half and remove the pit and skin and discard. Cut avocado flesh into ½-inch cubes and add to papaya and jicama. Add the lime vinaigrette and toss well to combine. Add cilantro, adjust seasoning, and toss again.

TURKEY and GREEN CHILE BURRITOS

serves 4

Turkey replaces the usual chicken or beef in this Mexican dish.

3 poblano peppers (about 8 ounces; see The Guide for sources)
1 medium onion, coarsely chopped
1 clove garlic, minced
1 tablespoon olive oil
½ fresh turkey breast (about 1¼ pounds), cut into 1-inch cubes
   Salt and freshly ground pepper
8 small red potatoes, unpeeled, cut into 1-inch cubes
1¾ cups low-sodium chicken stock

4 12-inch flour tortillas
4 ounces Monterey Jack cheese, grated

1. Roast poblanos on a fork directly over a gas flame, turning until all sides are charred, about 3 minutes. Set aside to cool in a plastic bag.
2. Heat oven to 350°. Cook onions ar garlic in olive oil in a deep skillet ⌐ medium-low heat until translucent, minutes. Add turkey, raise heat to ⌐ and cook until meat is golden ⌐ 6 minutes. Season; add potato⌐ Reduce heat to medium l⌐ simmer until potatoes⌐ cooked, 10 to 12 minut⌐ heat to medium; cook ⌐ to 10 minutes. Peel and seed ⌐ in strips, and add to mixture.
3. Place a quarter of the mixture on a ⌐ tilla, midway between the center and the edge near you. Scatter a quarter of the cheese over mixture. Fold right and left sides of tortilla over the filling and roll up tortilla away from you. Repeat with remaining tortillas, place in a baking dish, cover with foil, and bake to heat through, about 15 minutes.

COFFEE CUSTARD

serves 4

Serve this dessert warm or chilled.

   Butter, melted, for custard cups
1 cup heavy cream
½ cup whole milk
2 tablespoons instant espresso powder
3 large egg yolks
1 large egg
¼ cup sugar
1 teaspoon vanilla extract
¼ cup dark chocolate shavings (about 1 ounce)

1. Heat oven to 300°. Place a roasting pan three-quarters full of hot water in the oven. Brush four 6-ounce custard cups with butter and set aside.

...stard gets its ...n a water

2. Combine cream, milk, and espresso in a small saucepan and scald.
3. Whisk together egg yolks, egg, sugar, vanilla, and a pinch of salt in a medium bowl. Add a little of the hot milk mixture to the egg mixture and whisk well. Add the remaining milk mixture and whisk again to combine well. Strain mixture through a sieve.
4. Pour into the custard cups and place in water bath in oven, making sure that the water comes three-quarters of the way up sides of cups. Bake until the custard is set, about 35 minutes.
5. Remove from oven and water bath and cool for about 20 minutes. Loosen custards with a knife and invert onto serving dishes; sprinkle with chocolate. Alternatively, refrigerate and turn out when needed.

NO POSTAGE NECESSARY IF MAILED IN THE UNITED STATES

OPPOSITE: The soft colors of the celadon plate and bone utensils are perfect foils for the turkey burritos.
THIS PAGE: A vegetable peeler is ideal for grating the chocolate over the coffee custard. The plate is a contemporary take on French faience.

summer

Summer is a time for slowing down, for simplifying our overextended lives. So when it comes to dinner, it's nice to know you can turn out a tempting meal that doesn't require hours in the kitchen. These recipes rely on ingredients that are fresh and readily available, with an emphasis on the fruits and vegetables that give summer its distinctive taste. Ripe red tomatoes, yellow squash, and yellow peppers mix with penne to create a vegetable ragout. Cucumbers are combined with mint in a refreshing chilled soup. And for dessert, sweet cavaillon melon is filled with ruby port; ripe, juicy peaches are served with cinnamon crème fraîche.

Summer is the season for eating outdoors, at the family picnic table or while reclining on a blanket at the beach. It's also the season for grilling: Salmon with sweet hot mustard on toasted sourdough bread makes an elegant alternative to hamburgers. Tangy marinated chicken, quickly grilled then topped with a citrus salsa, is accompanied by homey cheddar biscuits.

You'll find most of what you need at the local farm stand, the butcher, and the fish market. Add them to the staples you have on hand, and dinner is on its way.

1

MANGO and TOMATO SALAD
with BASIL CURRY DRESSING

PENNE with SUMMER
VEGETABLE RAGOUT

FRESH PEACHES with
CINNAMON CREME FRAICHE

OATMEAL LACE COOKIES

PREPARATION SCHEDULE

1 Make and bake cookies.

2 Prepare vegetable ragout and keep warm.

3 Prepare cinnamon crème fraîche.

4 Prepare salad.

5 Cook and drain pasta. Mix with vegetable ragout.

6 Serve dinner.

7 Put together peaches with topping and serve with cookies.

MANGO and TOMATO SALAD with BASIL CURRY DRESSING

serves 4

You can make this basil dressing in an electric chopper or with julienned basil, but it won't have the same beautiful green color.

4	ripe plum tomatoes
1	large ripe mango (see Note)
1½	tablespoons extra-virgin olive oil
1	teaspoon white wine vinegar
	Pinch of curry powder
4-6	large basil leaves
	Salt and freshly ground pepper to taste

1. Core the tomatoes and cut into ½-inch wedges. Cut the mango from the pit in ½-inch slices. Remove the skin with a small knife. Arrange alternating slices of mango and tomato on a plate.

2. Using a mortar and pestle, combine the olive oil, white wine vinegar, curry powder, basil leaves, and salt and pepper, pulverizing the basil leaves. Drizzle the dressing over the mangoes and tomatoes and serve immediately.

NOTE: *If in doubt about the ripeness of a mango, buy a nice firm one and keep it in a closed paper bag for several days, until it gives off a fruity aroma and no longer feels firm.*

PENNE with SUMMER VEGETABLE RAGOUT

serves 4

These ingredients are only suggestions; use whatever's ripest, from the market or your garden.

2	cups diced eggplant
2	sprigs fresh rosemary
¼	cup olive oil
1	cup diced yellow squash
1	cup diced zucchini
	Salt and freshly ground pepper to taste
1	medium bulb fennel, thinly sliced (about 1 cup)
2	cups thinly sliced red onion
6	cloves garlic, peeled and smashed
1	red pepper, seeded and cut into small pieces
1	yellow pepper, seeded and cut into small pieces
1	tablespoon chopped fresh thyme
1	tablespoon freshly grated orange zest
2	cups seeded, diced ripe tomatoes
¼	cup balsamic vinegar
10	ounces penne

1. In a large pan over high heat, sauté eggplant and rosemary in oil for 5 minutes. Add squash and zucchini and sauté a few minutes more. Salt and pepper lightly. Add fennel, onion, and garlic and sauté until soft. Add peppers, reduce heat, and cook for 4 minutes. Mix in thyme and orange zest; add tomatoes and vinegar. Cook for 5 minutes. Remove from heat and adjust seasonings with salt, pepper, vinegar, or oil. Cover and keep warm.

2. Bring a large pot of salted water to a boil and add penne. Cook until tender. Rinse and toss with the vegetables. Serve hot or cold.

Cream-colored plates and a jacquard-weave tablecloth work well with this casual outdoor meal. An old tin grain measure filled with peaches serves as a centerpiece.

Not only are ripe summer peaches delicious, they're a good source of Vitamin A.

FRESH PEACHES with CINNAMON CRÈME FRAÎCHE

serves 4

Use the ripest freestone peaches you can find. For easier peeling, drop the peaches into boiling water for fifteen seconds, then plunge into ice water to cool.

½ cup crème fraîche (see Note)
2 tablespoons sugar
1 tablespoon cinnamon
4 peaches, peeled
   Mint sprigs, for garnish

Combine crème fraîche, sugar, and cinnamon. Divide evenly among four plates. Cut the peaches in half and arrange on top. Garnish with mint sprigs.

NOTE: *If you can't find crème fraîche, substitute plain yogurt and increase the sugar to 3 tablespoons.*

OATMEAL LACE COOKIES

makes about 25 three-inch cookies

Crisp and chewy at the same time, these southern delicacies are simple to make, and they keep well in an airtight container.

¾ pound (3 sticks) unsalted butter
3 cups uncooked rolled oats (do not use instant)
1½ tablespoons all-purpose flour
1 teaspoon salt
1¾ cups sugar
2 teaspoons vanilla extract
2 large eggs, lightly beaten

1. Heat oven to 325°. Cover a baking sheet with parchment paper.
2. In a large saucepan over low heat, melt the butter. Let cool a bit and add all remaining ingredients except the eggs. Stir well to combine, then add eggs. Mix until thoroughly incorporated.
3. Place 1½ teaspoons of batter at a time on the parchment, leaving at least 3 inches between cookies. Flatten batter into a circle with the back of a spoon. Bake for 13 to 15 minutes, or until just golden brown. Cool on wire racks.

A PEACH PRIMER

Peaches were first brought to North America in the sixteenth century, on Spanish ships. They thrived here, and today there are over two thousand peach varieties. Their colors range from porcelain to pale pink, from molten gold to crimson. They can be as sweet as raw sugar; tangy, with a taste of raspberry; or honeyed, with a hint of butterscotch.

Peaches come in two general types: those that are grown for canning (clingstone) and those for eating fresh (freestone). The flesh of a freestone breaks away from the pit without effort.

The differences in peach varieties have more to do with growing habits—when they ripen and where they grow—than with taste. Early-ripening varieties tend to have less flavor than those that mature later; however, all ripe peaches should be soft but firm. They should also be handled carefully, as they are easily bruised.

Peaches are very versatile: They can be made into chutney, ice cream, cobblers, and pies. But perhaps the best way to eat a peach is in its natural state, when the flesh almost melts in your mouth and the juices run down your chin.

AVOCADO and JICAMA SALAD

serves 4

Buy green, pebbly-skinned Haas avocados and let them ripen in a brown bag for a few days. When the skin turns black, they are ready to use.

1 small jicama
2 ripe avocados
Juice of 1 lemon
3 tablespoons balsamic vinegar
6 tablespoons extra-virgin olive oil
Salt and freshly ground pepper
½ small red onion, minced

1. Peel the jicama by cutting a thin slice off the top and bottom and paring sides with a small knife. Cut the jicama into ¼-inch-thick slices, then cut the slices into thin strips. Set aside.

2. Cut avocados in half lengthwise. Insert the blade of a heavy knife in pit, twist to remove, and discard. Peel avocado halves. Squeeze lemon juice over avocados to prevent browning; set aside.

3. Whisk together vinegar, oil, and salt and pepper to taste.

4. Make a bed of jicama on four plates, and top each with an avocado half. Season lightly with salt and pepper, sprinkle with onion, and pour dressing into avocado cavities. The salad will dress itself when you cut into avocados.

2

AVOCADO and JICAMA SALAD

CHEDDAR BISCUITS

GRILLED CHICKEN with
CITRUS SALSA

SUMMER BERRY GRATIN

PREPARATION SCHEDULE

1 Marinate chicken.

2 Prepare custard for gratin and refrigerate until chilled.

3 Prepare citrus salsa.

4 Prepare biscuit dough and cut biscuits.

5 Finish assembling berry gratins; do not bake.

6 Bake biscuits; prepare salads.

7 Grill chicken and arrange on greens with salsa.

8 Serve dinner.

9 Brown the berry gratins and serve.

LEFT: The avocado and jicama salad is served on a 1920s Sinclair plate.

GRILLED CHICKEN with CITRUS SALSA

serves 4

If you don't have a grill, sauté the chicken in a hot cast-iron skillet.

¼ cup plus 1 tablespoon fresh lime juice
¼ cup plus 1 tablespoon olive oil
2 jalapeño peppers, 1 thinly sliced, 1 diced
4 boneless chicken breasts, trimmed of fat and skin
Salt and freshly ground pepper
2 dashes tequila (optional)
1 navel orange, peeled, sectioned, and cut into ¼-inch pieces
1 small pink grapefruit, peeled, sectioned, and cut into ¼-inch pieces
4 scallions, thinly sliced
10 yellow and/or red cherry tomatoes, seeded and diced
Grated zests of ½ orange and ½ lime
¼ cup chopped fresh cilantro
4 tomatillos, diced (optional)
4 handfuls of mesclun or other mixed greens

1. In a shallow bowl, combine ¼ cup each of the lime juice and oil and the jalapeño slices. Rub chicken with salt and pepper; add to marinade. Add a dash of tequila. Marinate for at least half an hour.

2. In a medium bowl, combine citrus fruit, scallions, tomatoes, remaining lime juice and olive oil, zests, salt and pepper, diced jalapeño, cilantro, tomatillos, and remaining tequila. Set aside.

3. Remove chicken from marinade. Cook on a hot grill for about 5 minutes on each side, or until cooked through. Remove from grill and let stand 5 minutes.

4. Divide the greens among four plates. Slice the chicken and arrange on top of greens. Spoon salsa over each salad and serve immediately.

This table setting mixes periods and styles: a nineteenth-century cut-panel crystal wineglass and a Depression-glass plate. An Irish-linen table runner is used instead of a tablecloth.

ABOVE: Additional citrus salsa is served on the side in a yellow pressed-glass compote.

ABOVE RIGHT: Wrapping the cheddar biscuits in an Irish linen dish towel keeps them warm at the table.

CHEDDAR BISCUITS

makes 12 to 16

These tender biscuits are best eaten right from the oven. Adjust the cayenne pepper to your taste.

- 2 cups unbleached all-purpose flour
- 1 teaspoon salt
- 4 teaspoons baking powder
- ½ teaspoon cream of tartar
- 1 tablespoon sugar
- ½ teaspoon cayenne pepper
- 8 tablespoons (1 stick) unsalted butter
- 1 cup grated sharp cheddar cheese
- ⅔ cup milk

1. Heat oven to 425°. In a large bowl, thoroughly combine flour, salt, baking powder, cream of tartar, sugar, and cayenne.
2. Cut butter into pieces and work it in with your fingers until mixture is coarse and crumbly. Stir in cheese.
3. Make a well in center of flour mixture, pour in milk, and stir with a fork just until dough comes together. Do not overmix. Turn onto a lightly floured surface and knead gently 10 to 12 times.
4. Pat dough into a circle about ½ inch thick. Cut out biscuits using a floured 2-inch-round cutter. Do not twist cutter. Transfer biscuits to a lightly buttered baking sheet and bake for 12 to 15 minutes, or until brown. Serve hot.

SUMMER BERRY GRATIN

serves 4

Use four 4-inch gratin dishes for this custard, and make sure the broiler is fully heated before browning the tops.

- 1 tablespoon all-purpose flour
- 1 teaspoon cornstarch
- ¼ cup plus 1 tablespoon sugar
- 1 large egg plus 1 large egg yolk
- 1 cup milk
- ½ teaspoon vanilla extract
- 2 tablespoons unsalted butter
- ⅓ cup mascarpone cheese (Italian cream cheese)
- 1 pint mixed berries, such as raspberries, blackberries, blueberries Confectioners' sugar for tops

1. In a small bowl, sift together flour, cornstarch, and sugar.
2. In another bowl, beat the egg and yolk until pale and fluffy. Add dry ingredients slowly; beat until pale and fluffy again, about 2 minutes.
3. In a small, heavy-bottomed stainless-steel saucepan, scald milk. Slowly add half of it to egg-flour mixture, beating constantly. Add this mixture to remaining milk in saucepan, and cook over a very low flame, whisking constantly. When mixture bubbles and thickens, remove from heat and continue whisking for 1 minute. Transfer to a bowl and stir in vanilla and butter. Refrigerate until chilled. (The dessert can be prepared to this point up to 2 days ahead.)
4. Preheat broiler. Fold mascarpone into custard and divide among gratin dishes. Press berries into custard. Sift confectioners' sugar over tops and set on a cookie sheet. Broil on top rack until evenly browned, about 2 minutes. Let cool 1 minute and serve.

An individual summer berry gratin looks striking in an Apilco tartlet dish. The American damask square and the hand-blown Italian plate are from the 1920s.

RIGHT: For the cucumber soup, cups or mugs can be used in place of bowls.

FAR RIGHT: The apricots are served in an antique glass compote.

BELOW: For this informal dinner, an old marble-topped bistro table is set with blue-rimmed Leeds ware and cobalt-blue Depression-glass goblets.

3

CHILLED CUCUMBER
MINT SOUP

PASTA with
MARINATED TOMATOES

SEARED TUNA STEAKS
with CAPER BUTTER

CARAMELIZED APRICOTS
with ALMOND CREAM

PREPARATION SCHEDULE

1 Marinate tomatoes.

2 Prepare caper butter and refrigerate.

3 Marinate tuna.

4 Prepare soup and chill.

5 Prepare almond cream and refrigerate.

6 Cook pasta; grill fish.

7 Combine pasta with marinated tomatoes and serve dinner.

8 Prepare caramelized apricots, arrange with almond cream, and serve.

CHILLED CUCUMBER MINT SOUP

serves 4

A simple and refreshing summer starter, this soup takes only minutes to make.

- 4 cucumbers, peeled and seeded
- 1 small or ½ large clove garlic
- 1 cup plain yogurt, low-fat if desired
- 2 tablespoons fresh lemon juice, plus more to taste
- ¼ cup water
- 4 scallions, white and green parts, cut into 1-inch pieces
- ¾ cup fresh mint leaves, loosely packed
  Salt and freshly ground pepper

1. Cut one of the cucumbers into small dice and set aside for garnish. Cut the others into large chunks. Combine cucumber chunks, garlic, yogurt, lemon juice, and water in a blender and puree until smooth.
2. Add the scallions and mint leaves, reserving some of the mint for garnish, and puree briefly. Season with salt and pepper, and add more lemon juice if a tarter flavor is desired.
3. Chill until ready to serve. Stir well before serving, and ladle into bowls or mugs, garnishing each serving with a big spoonful of diced cucumber and a sprig of mint.

PASTA with MARINATED TOMATOES

serves 4

Sun-dried tomatoes add a smoky flavor to this simple sauce. Garganelle and penne rigate are both quill-shaped pastas that hold a thick sauce well.

- 2 large ripe tomatoes, seeded and coarsely chopped
- 4 oil-packed sun-dried tomatoes, drained and coarsely chopped
- 1 clove garlic, chopped
- ¼ cup extra-virgin olive oil
  Salt and freshly ground pepper

- ½ pound garganelle or penne rigate
- 1 cup fresh basil leaves, loosely packed

1. Combine fresh and sun-dried tomatoes, garlic, oil, salt, and pepper in a large bowl. Marinate at room temperature for 45 minutes, stirring occasionally.
2. Boil pasta in salted water until al dente, 7 to 10 minutes. Drain well, and while still hot, toss with tomato mixture.
3. Coarsely chop the basil and combine with pasta. Serve immediately or at room temperature.

SEARED TUNA STEAKS with CAPER BUTTER

serves 4

The tuna can also be cooked on the grill, but make sure it's very hot, so that the outside of the tuna is seared before the inside is cooked through.

- 4 fresh tuna steaks, each about 8 ounces and ¾-inch thick
  Extra-virgin olive oil, to coat tuna
  Salt and freshly ground pepper
- 4 tablespoons (½ stick) unsalted butter, at room temperature
- 2 tablespoons capers, rinsed and dried
- 1 tablespoon finely diced red and/or yellow bell pepper
- 1 large bunch fresh arugula

1. Rub the tuna with olive oil, salt, and plenty of pepper. Set aside to marinate for at least 20 minutes.
2. In a small bowl, combine butter, capers, and diced peppers. Turn mixture onto a square of parchment or waxed paper and roll into a log about ½ inch in diameter. Refrigerate until firm, about 30 minutes.
3. Heat an iron skillet slowly over low heat until very hot (a few drops of water splashed in the pan should evaporate almost immediately). Arrange tuna in skillet and cook for about 5 minutes on each side.

It should be well browned and crisp on the outside and rare to medium on the inside.
4. Arrange arugula on plates or platter. Place tuna on top with a slice of caper butter on each steak. Serve immediately.

CARAMELIZED APRICOTS with ALMOND CREAM

serves 4

Cook the fruit quickly, so that a layer of brittle caramel encases the soft interior. This recipe works just as well with peaches.

- ½ pint heavy cream
- 2 tablespoons confectioners' sugar
- 1 tablespoon amaretto or ½ teaspoon almond extract
- 4 tablespoons (½ stick) unsalted butter
- ¾ cup granulated sugar
- 8 apricots, ripe but firm, halved and pitted
- ¼ cup milk
- ¼ cup sliced almonds, toasted (optional)

1. Whip cream with confectioners' sugar until soft peaks form. Whisk in the amaretto or almond extract. Refrigerate until ready to use.
2. Melt butter in a large sauté pan over medium heat. Add sugar; stir to dissolve. Swirl occasionally until mixture is light brown, 3 to 5 minutes.
3. Add apricots, cut sides down. Increase heat to medium high, and cook until sugar has turned a deep amber and apricots are well caramelized, no more than 5 minutes. Shake pan a few times.
4. Remove pan from heat and, using a slotted spoon, transfer the apricots to a plate, cut sides up. Whisk milk into sugar mixture to make the caramel sauce. Simmer over low heat until thick, 2 to 3 minutes.
5. Arrange the apricots on four plates and pour caramel sauce over each one. Spoon the almond cream on the side and garnish with sliced almonds.

4

SUMMER GREEN ANTIPASTO

TOMATO BASIL COMPOTE

GRILLED PORK SKEWERS
with COUSCOUS

MELON with RUBY PORT

PREPARATION SCHEDULE

1 Marinate pork.

2 Prepare antipasto; keep cool.

3 Prepare couscous.

4 Heat grill; thread skewers; cook pork.

5 Prepare tomato-basil compote.

6 Halve and seed melons; add port.

SUMMER GREEN ANTIPASTO

serves 4

Ricotta salata is a dry cheese available in Italian markets. If you can't find it, try pecorino or feta instead.

2 pounds unshelled fava beans (about 24 pods)

1 lemon

6 inner stalks celery, plus hearts, peeled and cut into 4-by-½-inch sticks

2 sprigs flat-leaf parsley, coarsely chopped, plus 2 more sprigs for garnish

8 ounces ricotta salata, sliced ½ inch thick

2 heads Belgian endive, leaves separated

½ cup picholine or other green olives (about 3 ounces)

1. Split fava-bean pods lengthwise with your fingers and remove beans. Bring a saucepan of water to a boil and add beans. Cook for 10 seconds, drain, and plunge into a bowl of ice water. Drain; peel one end of each bean and squeeze gently to pop bean from skin. Discard skins. Set beans aside.

2. Cut lemon in half and squeeze over celery. Sprinkle with chopped parsley. Arrange beans, celery, cheese, endive leaves, and olives on a serving platter and garnish with parsley sprigs.

TOMATO BASIL COMPOTE

serves 4

Heat plumps the tiny tomatoes, creating a luscious compote to top grilled foods or serve as a side dish.

1½ tablespoons olive oil

2 cloves garlic, peeled and thinly sliced

1½ pints mixed yellow, red, and orange pear and cherry tomatoes
Salt and freshly ground pepper

8 large basil leaves

Heat oil in a large skillet over medium-low heat. Add garlic and cook until soft and golden, about 3 minutes. Add tomatoes, season well with salt and pepper, and cook, stirring often, until tomatoes are just warm and ready to burst, 3 to 5 minutes. Add basil and cook until just wilted, about 1 minute. Spoon compote over pork skewers.

GRILLED PORK SKEWERS
with COUSCOUS

serves 4

The honey-mustard marinade tenderizes and adds flavor to the pork.

1 teaspoon Dijon mustard

1 teaspoon honey

Juice of 1 lemon

1 tablespoon fresh thyme (about 4 sprigs), plus more for garnish
Salt and freshly ground pepper

2½ tablespoons olive oil, plus more to brush on grill

2 cloves garlic, peeled and finely chopped

1¼ pounds pork tenderloin, trimmed and cut into 1-inch cubes

½ medium red onion, cut into ¼-inch dice

½ each small zucchini and yellow squash, cut into ¼-inch dice

1 each red and yellow peppers, seeded and cut into ¼-inch dice

1 cup dry couscous

1 cup boiling water

1. Mix first 4 ingredients, salt, pepper, 1 tablespoon oil, and half the garlic in a large bowl. Add pork and cover; let stand for at least ½ hour.

2. Heat remaining oil in a saucepan over medium-low heat. Add remaining garlic and the onion. Cook until translucent, about 4 minutes; add vegetables, raise heat, and cook until just soft, about 5 minutes more. Add couscous and water; stir well. Turn off heat, cover, and let sit for 5 minutes. Season with salt and pepper.

3. Heat grill and brush with oil. Thread pork on skewers; season with salt and pepper. Grill on each side until done. Serve over the couscous.

MELON with RUBY PORT

serves 4

A perfectly ripe melon is aromatic and yields to firm pressure at the stem end.

2 small honeydew, cantaloupe, cavaillon, or other orange-fleshed melons

½ cup ruby port

Cut melons in half and remove seeds with a spoon. Place each half in a bowl and pour 2 tablespoons port in the center.

The word antipasto (literally "before the pasta") refers to a selection of Italian appetizers, often including smoked meats and marinated vegetables. This vegetarian version is made with celery, fava beans, endive, and ricotta salata.

RIGHT: Serving wine in iridescent Depression-glass tumblers rather than wineglasses adds an informal touch.

BELOW: The pork skewers with couscous are presented on an ironstone platter before being served.

LEFT: A banded blue mixing bowl doubles as a serving dish for a warm compote of cherry tomatoes and basil.

54

A cavaillon melon is served in a footed bowl with a silver-plate citrus spoon. The center of the melon is filled with ruby port.

FAR LEFT: Tender green beans are tossed with ricotta salata and served in an ironstone dish.
LEFT: An ironstone ramekin is just the right size for serving the red pepper and lemon confit.

RED PEPPER and LEMON CONFIT

serves 4

If yellow and orange bell peppers are available, mix them to make a more colorful relish.

- 4 red bell peppers (about 1¾ pounds), seeds and ribs removed
- 1½ tablespoons olive oil
- 5 shallots (about 5 ounces), peeled and sliced into ¼-inch rounds
- 1 cup dry white wine
- ½ teaspoon salt
- ⅛ teaspoon freshly ground pepper
- 1 lemon

1. Cut peppers into thin strips. Heat the oil in a large skillet over medium-low heat. Add shallots and cook until they begin to brown, about 15 to 20 minutes. Add red peppers, wine, salt, and pepper. Cover and cook until wine is almost absorbed, about 20 minutes, stirring occasionally. Uncover and reduce heat to low. Cook, stirring occasionally, until peppers are tender, about 15 minutes.

2. Meanwhile, remove lemon zest in long thin strips and set aside. Use a small, sharp knife to cut away pith. Remove lemon sections by sliding the knife down one side of a section, cutting it away from the white membrane. Twist blade under section to lift it out. Remove all sections, cut them in half, and add to peppers along with zest. Toss to combine and serve.

GREEN BEANS with RICOTTA SALATA

serves 4

Plump, sweet green beans are a good source of vitamin A and potassium.

- 1 tablespoon plus ¼ teaspoon salt
- 1 pound string beans, stem ends trimmed
- 2 ounces ricotta salata, crumbled
- 20 small basil leaves
- ½ teaspoon Dijon mustard
- 1 tablespoon red-wine vinegar
- 3 tablespoons extra-virgin olive oil
- ⅛ teaspoon freshly ground pepper

1. Bring a large saucepan of cold water to a boil. Add 1 tablespoon salt and trimmed beans. Cook until the beans are just tender, about 4 minutes. Remove from the heat, drain, and immediately plunge the beans into an ice-water bath to stop the cooking process. Drain, pat the beans dry, and place in a large bowl along with the ricotta salata and basil leaves.

2. In a small bowl, whisk together mustard, vinegar, olive oil, remaining ¼ teaspoon salt, and pepper.

3. Pour the vinaigrette over bean mixture and toss well.

5

GREEN BEANS
with RICOTTA SALATA

SOFT-SHELL CRABS
with ARUGULA

RED PEPPER
and LEMON CONFIT

CHERRIES with KIRSCH
and SORBET

PREPARATION SCHEDULE

1 Prepare cherries.

2 Begin cooking confit.

3 Blanch beans and make vinaigrette.

4 Dredge and cook crabs.

5 Toss salad and serve dinner.

6 Serve dessert.

SOFT-SHELL CRABS
with ARUGULA

serves 4

When you buy soft-shell crabs, have them cleaned at the fish market.

- 1 cup yellow cornmeal
- 1 teaspoon salt
- ¼ teaspoon freshly ground pepper
- 2 large egg whites
- 8 soft-shell crabs (about 2½ pounds)
- 6 tablespoons olive oil
- 1 bunch arugula (about 6 ounces), washed and tough stems removed
  Red Pepper and Lemon Confit

1. Combine cornmeal, salt, and pepper in a shallow bowl or plate.

2. Whisk the egg whites in a small bowl until just frothy. Dip the crabs into the egg whites to coat. Dredge them in the seasoned cornmeal, shake off any excess, and set aside.

3. Heat 1½ tablespoons olive oil in a large nonstick skillet over medium-high heat; arrange 4 crabs on their bellies in the pan. Cook until golden and crisp, about 5 minutes. Transfer crabs to a plate and add 1½ tablespoons olive oil to pan. Return crabs to pan, on their backs, and cook until crisp, about 5 minutes more. Remove crabs from skillet and keep warm on a baking sheet in a 300° oven. Repeat with the remaining olive oil and crabs.

4. Divide arugula among four plates. Arrange two crabs over each plate of arugula, spoon confit over or around crabs, and serve.

CHERRIES with KIRSCH
and SORBET

serves 4

Use this simple recipe with other favorite fruits and sorbets.

- 1 pound fresh Bing cherries, halved and pitted
- 2 tablespoons kirsch
- 2 tablespoons sugar
- 1 pint lemon sorbet

1. In a small bowl, toss together cherries, kirsch, and sugar. Let stand for about 1 hour, until cherries soften and become juicy.

2. Place a large scoop of sorbet in each of four chilled wine goblets or dessert glasses. Spoon cherries over and serve immediately.

BELOW: Thick handblown tumblers stand up to a summer breeze, making them well-suited to outdoor dining.

OPPOSITE: Soft-shell crabs are available fresh from May through the middle of October.

THIS PAGE: Bing cherries are almost black when fully ripe. Here they're spooned over lemon sorbet and served in a candlewick cup.

RIGHT: Hot summer nights call for snack-sized foods like these ham-and-orange triangles. They're presented on a Leeds-ware-inspired dish.

BELOW: Spanish-style cucumber-and-feta-cheese tapa and paella salad look pretty on a fluted ironstone plate.

6

CUCUMBER TAPA

SPANISH HAM with
OLIVES and ORANGES

PAELLA SALAD

SANGRIA SOUP

PREPARATION SCHEDULE

1 Make and chill sangria soup.

2 Cook rice and squid;
prepare other ingredients for
paella salad and toss.

4 Prepare cucumber tapa.

5 Make ham, olive, and
orange tapa.

CUCUMBER TAPA

serves 4

*If possible, use European hothouse
cucumbers. They have fewer seeds and
are usually not waxed.*

2 cucumbers (about 1 pound each),
peeled if waxy

2 tablespoons extra-virgin olive oil

1 teaspoon sherry vinegar

2 ounces feta cheese, diced

¼ teaspoon salt
Pinch of freshly ground black pepper

1 tablespoon fresh oregano leaves,
coarsely chopped

1. Slice the cucumbers lengthwise; remove seeds. Cut 1 cucumber half into ¼-inch dice and transfer to a small bowl. Add the olive oil, vinegar, feta cheese, salt, and pepper and toss well. Add oregano and toss again.

2. Use a vegetable peeler to remove 1 or 2 long strips of peel (if cucumbers are already peeled, remove a strip of flesh) from the underside of each cucumber half so they will sit without tipping. Divide the cucumber-and-feta mixture among them.

3. Slice cucumbers on a slight diagonal into 1½-inch sections and serve immediately.

SPANISH HAM with OLIVES and ORANGES

serves 4

Serrano is a Spanish dry-cured ham; prosciutto can be substituted.

2 oranges
¼ cup imported green olives, such as Provençal, pitted
½ small shallot, sliced into very thin rounds
1 tablespoon olive oil
2 tablespoons fresh orange juice
1 teaspoon sherry vinegar
¼ teaspoon salt
  Pinch of freshly ground black pepper
1 10-inch-diameter round loaf of country bread (about 1 pound)
8 very thin slices serrano ham (about 2 ounces)

1. Remove zest from a quarter of 1 orange, cut zest into very thin strips; set aside.

2. Cut away peel and pith of oranges and separate segments, removing the white membranes. Cut segments into ½-inch pieces and place in a small bowl. Coarsely chop olives and add to oranges. Add shallot, olive oil, orange juice, vinegar, salt, and pepper; toss to combine.

3. Cut bread into 4 wedges. Split 1 wedge crosswise with your hands (set remaining bread aside for another use), separating the top and bottom crusts. Tear each half into 4 chunks and arrange on a serving plate. Place a slice of ham, folding or rolling it if necessary, on each piece of bread and spoon 1 tablespoon of the orange mixture on top. Sprinkle with zest and serve.

PAELLA SALAD

serves 4

This salad is a simple version of the classic Spanish dish.

½ teaspoon saffron
1 cup long-grain white rice
3 teaspoons salt
4 tablespoons fresh lime juice
2 tablespoons fresh orange juice
2 tablespoons extra-virgin olive oil
1 small clove garlic, minced
¼ teaspoon freshly ground pepper
1 teaspoon ground cumin
1 pound cleaned squid, bodies cut into ¼-inch rings
1½ cups quartered cherry tomatoes (12 ounces)
3 celery stalks, peeled and chopped into ¼-inch dice
¼ cup tightly packed cilantro leaves, roughly chopped

1. Crumble saffron into 2 cups of cold water in a medium saucepan with a tight-fitting lid. Stir in rice and 1 teaspoon salt; bring to a boil. Reduce heat to low, cover, and simmer until rice is tender, 12 to 15 minutes. Remove from heat and let stand, covered, for 10 minutes. Fluff rice and transfer to a bowl to cool.

2. Whisk together lime and orange juices, olive oil, garlic, 1 teaspoon salt, pepper, and cumin. Pour over cooled rice and mix to combine.

3. Bring a saucepan of cold water to a boil. Add remaining teaspoon salt and squid. Cook until squid is completely opaque, about 30 seconds. Drain and plunge into a bowl of ice water. Drain again, pat dry, and add to rice. Toss with remaining ingredients and serve.

SANGRIA SOUP

serves 4

Sangria is traditionally made with robust red table wine; for this chilled dessert soup, use a light, fruity red, such as a Beaujolais or a Valpolicella.

3 cups 2-inch watermelon chunks (about 2 pounds with rind), seeds and rind removed
¼ cup light, fruity red wine
1 tablespoon cranberry juice
  Juice of 1 lime (about 2 tablespoons)
2 tablespoons sugar
1 tablespoon honey
¼ honeydew melon, rind and seeds removed and cut into ½-inch pieces (about 1 cup)
¼ cantaloupe, rind and seeds removed and cut into ½-inch pieces (about 1 cup)
1 tablespoon coarsely chopped fresh mint leaves

1. Place 2 cups of the watermelon chunks in a medium bowl. Add the wine, cranberry juice, lime juice, sugar, and honey; let stand 15 minutes.

2. Cut remaining watermelon chunks into ½-inch pieces; set aside.

3. Transfer watermelon-and-wine mixture to a food processor and pulse until almost smooth, about 30 seconds. Return to bowl; add honeydew, cantaloupe, reserved watermelon, and mint leaves. Stir well, chill, and serve cold.

7

MIXED SUMMER BEAN SALAD

PARMESAN TOAST

CLAMS in RICH BROTH
with ORZO

PEACH SHORTCAKES

PREPARATION SCHEDULE

1 Scrub clams.
   Prepare bean salad.

2 Cut up onion, garlic, tomato,
   and herbs for clams.

3 Make Parmesan toast.

4 Slice peaches; sprinkle with
   liqueur and sugar.
   Prepare shortcakes.

5 Cook clams and orzo.

MIXED SUMMER BEAN SALAD

serves 4

*Use any combination of fresh beans you like.
They can be cooked ahead of time and refrigerated until you're ready to use them.*

1 pound mixed fresh beans, such as
   string beans, wax beans, haricots
   verts, and shelled fava beans
1 shallot, peeled and finely diced
3 tablespoons extra-virgin olive oil
   Salt and freshly ground pepper
   Red-wine vinegar
   Chopped fresh herbs, such as
   tarragon, basil, or parsley (optional)
8 leaves red-leaf lettuce

1. Trim stem ends of beans. Bring a large
pot of salted water to a boil. Blanch each
type of bean separately until crisp-tender.
Refresh in ice water, drain, and pat dry.
2. Toss beans with shallot, oil, and salt
and pepper to taste. Add vinegar to taste
and herbs, if desired.
3. Arrange red-leaf lettuce and beans on
each of 4 plates, and serve.

CLAMS in RICH BROTH
with ORZO

serves 4

*Place a dish in the middle of the
table for empty shells.*

2 tablespoons olive oil, plus more
   for drizzling
2-4 cloves garlic, peeled and thinly sliced
1 large onion, peeled and sliced
2 dried red chile peppers
1 cup white wine
1 cup chicken stock or water
2 tablespoons unsalted butter
   Salt
5 pounds littleneck or Manila clams,
   scrubbed well
¼ cup chopped tomato
1 tablespoon each chopped fresh
   parsley and basil
1 pound orzo (rice-shaped pasta)

1. In a large, heavy pot, heat oil over medium heat. Add garlic and cook until golden
brown, 2 to 3 minutes. Add onion and
chile peppers and cook until onion is soft,
5 to 7 minutes.
2. Add wine and bring to a boil. Add stock
or water and boil for 5 minutes. Add butter, salt to taste, clams, and tomato, and
cover. Cook, stirring occasionally, for 15 to
20 minutes, or until all clams have opened
(discard any that haven't). Stir in herbs.
3. Meanwhile, bring a large pan of water
to a boil. Add orzo and a pinch of salt;
cook until al dente. Drain and drizzle with
a little oil.
4. Spoon a serving of orzo in each of 4 large
bowls, add enough broth just to cover, and
arrange clams around edge of each bowl.

LEFT: Yellow English ironstone dessert
plates can also be used for the mixed
summer bean salad.

The clams and orzo are served in vibrant oversized earthenware bowls.

Clams are members of the bi-valve family, which also includes mussels, oysters, and scallops. Clams have either hard or soft shells, and are found in tidal flats on both coasts, although most commercial production is in the East.

Hard-shell clams, which are sold by the dozen, are graded by size: littlenecks (also known as Manila clams) are the smallest, followed by cherrystone, chowder, and quahog. Soft-shell clams, on the other hand, are not sorted by size and are sold by the pound. As a rule, the smallest are steamers (also known as gapers); razor and horse clams are bigger, and the enormous geoduck is the largest of all. In general, the smaller the clam, the more tender the meat.

Clams in their shells must be sold live; hard-shell clams should be tightly closed. To clean hard-shell clams, scrub them with a stiff brush under running water. Any clams that haven't opened after cooking should be discarded.

Soft-shell clams are never eaten raw. If you've gathered them yourself, they may contain large quantities of sand that need to be purged. Rinse them in water a few times, then soak them for several hours in salted or seawater. Rinse them again, then cook as desired.

ABOVE: Make sure to allow for at least two Parmesan toasts per person.

PARMESAN TOAST

serves 4

Parmigiano-Reggiano is the best cheese to use for these.

1 thin, crusty baguette
2 tablespoons unsalted butter (optional)
1 clove garlic, peeled
1 cup coarsely grated Parmesan

1. Heat oven to 400°. Cut baguette at a sharp angle into 1½-inch slices. Spread both sides with butter, if desired, and place on a baking sheet.
2. Toast in oven until golden brown, 3 to 4 minutes on each side.
3. Rub garlic clove on one side of each toast and top with a sprinkling of cheese. Return to oven and toast until cheese is crisp and golden brown, 8 to 10 minutes. Turn heat down to 350° if toast begins to brown too fast. Serve warm or at room temperature.

PEACH SHORTCAKES

serves 4

Blanch the peaches in boiling water to remove the skins, if you like.

4 ripe peaches
1 tablespoon kirsch or peach schnapps (optional)
1 tablespoon granulated sugar, plus more for sprinkling tops
2 cups all-purpose flour
1 tablespoon baking powder
4 tablespoons dark brown sugar
½ teaspoon salt
6 tablespoons (¾ stick) chilled unsalted butter, cut into pieces
¼-½ cup heavy cream or milk, plus more for brushing tops
1 cup heavy cream, whipped with ½ teaspoon vanilla extract

1. Heat oven to 400°. Slice peaches; sprinkle with kirsch or schnapps, if desired, and 1 tablespoon granulated sugar. Set aside.
2. In the bowl of a food processor, combine the rest of the dry ingredients. Add butter and process with on-off pulses until the mixture resembles coarse meal. Add cream or milk slowly, pulsing until the dough comes together.
3. Turn out dough onto a lightly floured board and knead once or twice. Pat into a ¾-inch-thick square. Trim edges and cut into 4 squares. Brush with additional cream or milk; sprinkle with sugar.
4. Place on a lightly oiled baking sheet; bake for 20 to 25 minutes.
5. Let shortcakes cool slightly, then split horizontally. Place bottom halves on dessert plates, and top with peaches and whipped cream. Cover with top halves of shortcakes, and serve.

Almost any fruit can be made into a shortcake dessert. Here, ripe peaches are sliced and topped with vanilla-flavored whipped cream. The goblets are handblown crystal.

TOMATO-POTATO SALAD
with BASIL

serves 4

The potatoes taste best hot off the grill with the cool tomatoes, but they can also be served at room temperature.

4-6 red potatoes (about 1 pound), cut into ¼-inch-thick slices
Extra-virgin olive oil
Salt and freshly ground pepper
2-3 large, ripe tomatoes (enough for 12 slices)
16 fresh basil leaves, half green and half purple basil, if available
Balsamic vinegar

1. Brush potato slices lightly with oil and sprinkle with salt and pepper. Place on a medium-hot grill and cook, covered, 3 to 5 minutes on each side, or until tender.
2. Slice tomatoes and arrange on plates along with potatoes, tucking basil leaves among them.
3. Drizzle with vinegar and additional oil, and sprinkle with salt and pepper to taste.

LOBSTER on the GRILL

serves 4

If you're not squeamish, the lobsters can also be killed by inserting the point of a sharp knife through the cross mark on their backs.

4 live lobsters, 1 to 2 pounds each
Melted butter (optional)
Lemon wedges

1. Kill lobsters by plunging them headfirst into salted boiling water and cooking for 1 minute. Remove and drain.
2. Place lobsters on a medium-hot grill. Cook for 8 to 10 minutes, turning occasionally to avoid burning the shells.
3. Crack a claw to see if it is fully cooked (the meat should be opaque). If not, detach claws and return to grill for a few minutes more. Using kitchen scissors, split

8

TOMATO-POTATO SALAD
with BASIL

LOBSTER on the GRILL

GRILLED VEGETABLES
and TOMATO BREAD

FRUIT with RICOTTA
and PLUM SAUCE

PREPARATION SCHEDULE

1 Make plum sauce for dessert.
2 Light grill; heat until coals are gray and ashy.
3 Prepare vegetables and bread for grilling.
4 Slice potatoes for salad and grill.

lobsters lengthwise by cutting along underside of tail, leaving back of shell intact. Scrape out red coral, if any, and green tomalley; combine with melted butter for a dipping sauce, if desired. Keep lobsters warm on a platter covered with foil until ready to serve. Garnish with lemon wedges.

GRILLED VEGETABLES
and TOMATO BREAD

serves 4

The softened grilled garlic is delicious spread on the tomato bread.

1 head garlic
1 red onion, peeled and thickly sliced
Olive oil
1 medium eggplant or 2 baby

eggplants, purple or white
2 zucchini, cut in half lengthwise
2 yellow squash, cut in half lengthwise
1 yellow bell pepper, seeded and quartered
1 red bell pepper, seeded and quartered
1 loaf of crusty bread
1 tomato
1 bunch arugula

1. Brush garlic and onion slices and place near the edge of a me grill to cook slowly. Grill for 5 to utes, turning garlic often. Leave while cooking vegetables in step 2.
2. Cut eggplant into thick slices or in half lengthwise, depending on size. Brush eggplant, zucchini, yellow squash, and peppers lightly with oil; place in center of grill. Cook a few minutes per side, turning once, until vegetables are seared and brown.
3. Slice bread and brush with oil. Grill on both sides just until brown. Cut tomato in half and rub over one side of hot bread; discard tomato.
4. Arrange grilled vegetables, bread, onion, and garlic on top of arugula and serve immediately.

BELOW: The tomato-potato salad uses two types of basil: green and the milder 'Purple Ruffles.'

FRUIT with RICOTTA and PLUM SAUCE

serves 4

*Summer fruit at its peak needs only a little
embellishment to make an elegant dessert.*

2	purple plums, quartered and pitted
½	cup water
2	tablespoons sugar
¼	teaspoon cinnamon
8	ounces fresh ricotta
1	tablespoon honey, plus more for drizzling
	Mixed summer fruit, such as white peaches, figs, strawberries, red and white cherries, blackberries, and blueberries
	Fresh mint, for garnish

1. To make plum sauce, place plums in a
saucepan with the water, sugar, and cinnamon. Simmer until fruit has broken down
and become mostly liquid, about 10 to 15
minutes. Put through a strainer, and adjust
sugar to taste. Let cool.

2. Place the ricotta in a bowl and stir in the
honey. Drizzle more honey over the surface
of the cheese.

3. Wash and cut the fruit into serving-size
pieces. Arrange on a platter and garnish
with mint. Serve with the plum sauce and
ricotta on the side.

9

HEARTS of BIBB SALAD

SUMMER SLAW with
POPPY SEED DRESSING

GRILLED SALMON SANDWICH
with SWEET HOT MUSTARD

BERRIES MACERATED in
KIRSCH with MINT

PREPARATION SCHEDULE

1 Macerate berries.
2 Prepare dressing and vegetables
   for slaw.
3 Prepare vinaigrette and lettuce
   for salad.
4 Make mustard sauce;
   wash arugula.
5 Grill salmon; dress salad;
   toss slaw.
6 Toast bread; assemble
   sandwiches; serve dinner.
7 Garnish berries and serve.

LEFT: This crispy summer slaw is served in a ceramic Russel Wright bowl. From the 1930s through the 1960s, Wright was known for his pared-down, practical designs.

SUMMER SLAW with POPPY SEED DRESSING

serves 4

Fennel, green beans, and poppy seeds make for an unexpected variation on traditional coleslaw.

    3 tablespoons crème fraîche or
       sour cream
       1½-inch piece fresh ginger,
       peeled and grated
    2½ tablespoons fresh orange juice
    1 scant teaspoon poppy seeds
       Salt and freshly ground pepper
    2 small carrots
    1 small bulb (about ½ pound) fennel
    ¼ pound green beans, trimmed

1. In a small bowl, whisk together the crème fraîche or sour cream, ginger, orange juice, and half the poppy seeds. Season to taste with salt and pepper. Refrigerate until needed.
2. Peel and julienne carrots. Slice fennel bulb crosswise, as thinly as possible. Cut beans into long strips. Combine vegetables in a medium bowl and toss with dressing immediately before serving. Garnish with remaining poppy seeds.

HEARTS of BIBB SALAD

serves 4

A head of Bibb lettuce usually yields the right amount for one person.

    1 medium tomato, cored, seeded,
       and coarsely chopped
    ½ cucumber, peeled, seeded,
       and coarsely chopped
    3 teaspoons sherry vinegar
    2 tablespoons extra-virgin olive oil
       Salt and freshly ground pepper
    ¼ cup coarsely chopped flat-leaf
       parsley
    4 heads Bibb lettuce, with outer
       leaves removed, quartered
    2 ounces Roquefort, crumbled

1. In a small mixing bowl, combine tomato and cucumber. Toss with vinegar and olive oil and season with salt and pepper. Allow to sit for 15 minutes. Stir in parsley.
2. Arrange lettuce hearts on plates and top with tomato mixture and cheese. Season with additional fresh pepper if desired.

Bibb lettuce, mild and buttery tasting,
goes well with tangy Roquefort. Both
the knife and four-prong fork are
English silver.

A grilled-salmon sandwich is served on a dinner plate from Russel Wright's Highlight collection.

GRILLED SALMON SANDWICH
with SWEET HOT MUSTARD

serves 4

Flat, wide fillets cut from the tail of the salmon work well for this open-face sandwich.

 2 tablespoons dry mustard
 3 tablespoons brown sugar
 ½ teaspoon soy sauce
 3 teaspoons olive oil
 4 salmon fillets, about 6 ounces each
    Salt and freshly ground pepper
 ½ bunch arugula, leaves slightly wet
 4 slices sourdough bread,
    crust trimmed

1. Combine mustard and sugar in a small bowl. Stir in 1½ tablespoons water. Add soy sauce and 1 teaspoon oil. Set aside.
2. Heat a grill or grill pan until very hot. Brush salmon with remaining oil; season with salt and pepper. Grill for 5 minutes, or until browned. Turn and cook for another 5 minutes, or to desired doneness.
3. Heat a small skillet over medium heat and add arugula. Season with salt and pepper, and cover. Cook until wilted, tossing leaves occasionally, about 2 minutes.
4. Toast bread and place on plates. Top each with wilted arugula and a salmon fillet. Drizzle the mustard sauce over top. Serve immediately.

BERRIES MACERATED in
KIRSCH WITH MINT

serves 4

Kirsch, a cherry brandy, heightens the flavor of fresh fruit.

 ½   pint (about 1 cup) raspberries
 ½   pint (about 1 cup) blackberries
 ½   pint (about 1 cup) blueberries
 8   large strawberries, stems removed,
     sliced lengthwise
 1½ tablespoons sugar, or to taste
 3   tablespoons kirsch
 3   sprigs fresh mint

Combine fruit in a small mixing bowl and toss with sugar and kirsch. Refrigerate until needed, at least one hour, tossing occasionally. Transfer to a serving bowl and garnish with torn mint leaves.

Raspberries, blackberries, blueberries, and sliced strawberries are soaked in a nineteenth-century Scandinavian glass bowl (above left), then brought to the table in an earthenware Japanese tea bowl (above).

autumn

Autumn—that all-too-brief interlude between summer vacation and winter holidays—is the ideal season for trying out new recipes. Take advantage of this time to linger over dinner with family and friends, or to indulge in one last meal outdoors before the weather turns too cold.

Autumn's extraordinary color and flavor palettes are reflected in these menus: Butternut squash gives pale white risotto an orange glow, and mixed greens are splashed with apple-cider vinaigrette. Beets, in red, yellow, orange, and white, make a sweet starter. Russet-tinged pears are cooked with onions in a warm salad; for dessert, they're glazed with golden maple syrup.

Cooler days also bring with them a desire for meals that are more substantial: Potatoes are combined with herbs and mashed, or baked with cheese in a cream-free gratin. Pancetta, Italian bacon, adds depth to penne and tomatoes, and Cornish hens are served with a kasha-and-pasta pilaf.

Apples, perhaps the ultimate autumn fruit, are cooked with sugar and spices then rolled in sheets of phyllo dough. For a more indulgent finale, individual warm brownie cups and sugar-dusted mocha shortbread wedges will please even the most devoted chocolate lover.

ABOVE: These sturdy greens stand up to the tart dressing.

AUTUMN GREENS with CIDER VINAIGRETTE

serves 4

The cider and cider vinegar add an unusual and unexpected tang to the vinaigrette.

- 1 shallot, minced
- 1 tablespoon apple cider
- 2 tablespoons apple-cider vinegar
- ¼ cup walnut oil
  Salt and freshly ground pepper
- 5 cups mixed greens, such as Belgian endive, Swiss chard, watercress, and romaine

In a small bowl, whisk together shallot, cider, and vinegar. Whisk in the walnut oil, and season to taste with salt and pepper. Toss with the greens and divide among four plates. Serve immediately.

SKILLET BRAISED FENNEL

serves 4

Fresh fennel, which has a strong anise flavor and crunchy texture when raw, becomes mellow and meltingly soft when braised.

- 4 medium bulbs fennel
- 1½ tablespoons unsalted butter
- 1 teaspoon sugar
- 1-2 cloves garlic, sliced thin
- ¼ cup fresh orange juice
- 1 cup water
  Salt and freshly ground pepper
  Flat-leaf parsley leaves, as garnish

1. Trim the tops of the fennel bulbs; cut bulbs in half lengthwise.
2. Melt butter in a large iron skillet over medium heat. Add sugar and stir until melted. Add garlic and cook for 1 to 2 minutes. Add fennel, cut side down, and cook until well browned, about 5 to 10 minutes. Be careful not to let the fennel burn.

1

AUTUMN GREENS with
CIDER VINAIGRETTE

SKILLET-BRAISED FENNEL

BUTTERNUT SQUASH RISOTTO

WARM BROWNIE CUPS

PREPARATION SCHEDULE

1 Steam squash for risotto, mash, and reserve.

2 Wash and dry greens for salad; prepare vinaigrette.

3 Prepare brownie cups; reserve without baking.

4 Braise fennel.

5 Prepare risotto.

6 Toss greens with vinaigrette.

7 Put brownie cups in oven to bake.

8 Serve dinner.

9 Dust brownie cups with confectioners' sugar; serve dessert.

3. Turn over bulbs and add orange juice, water, and salt and pepper. Bring to a simmer, then reduce heat to low. Cover pan and cook until fennel is soft and most of the liquid has been absorbed, about 20 to 30 minutes. If the pan becomes dry during cooking, add a little more water. If any liquid is left at the end of the cooking time, continue to cook, uncovered, at medium heat until the liquid evaporates. Garnish with parsley leaves and serve immediately.

BUTTERNUT SQUASH RISOTTO

serves 4 to 6

Though it may seem arduous, constant stirring gives risotto its creamy texture.

1 medium butternut squash

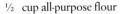

2 cups Arborio rice
½ cup dry white wine
  Freshly grated nutmeg
  Salt and freshly ground pepper
1 tablespoon chopped fresh rosemary, plus sprigs for garnish
½ cup freshly grated Parmesan

1. Cut squash into eighths and discard the seeds. Steam squash for 10 to 15 minutes or until tender. Scoop the flesh from the skin and mash lightly.
2. In a large saucepan, heat stock to a simmer. In a large, heavy saucepan over medium heat, melt 1 tablespoon butter. Add oil and shallots; cook for 2 minutes. Add rice; cook, stirring, for 5 minutes.
3. Add wine to rice and cook, stirring, until wine is nearly absorbed. Stir in a cup of stock and the squash; simmer until liquid is nearly absorbed. Continue stirring in stock, a ladleful at a time, until rice is creamy and firm but not hard in the center, 15 to 20 minutes. Add nutmeg and salt and pepper to taste. Add chopped rosemary. Stir in the remaining butter and most of the Parmesan. Serve in shallow bowls garnished with the remaining cheese and rosemary sprigs.

WARM BROWNIE CUPS

makes 5

Bake this puddinglike dessert in individual custard cups or ramekins.

4 ounces semisweet chocolate
8 tablespoons (1 stick) unsalted butter

½ cup all-purpose flour
½ teaspoon baking powder
  Pinch of salt
½ cup cocoa powder
4 large eggs, at room temperature
1 teaspoon vanilla extract
1 cup sugar
  Confectioners' sugar, for dusting

1. Heat oven to 350°. Place a baking pan half full of water in oven.
2. Bring a saucepan of water to barely simmering. Place chocolate and butter in a heatproof bowl. Place over water and stir until almost melted. Remove bowl from heat and let cool, stirring occasionally.
3. Sift together twice all the dry ingredients except sugar. Set aside.
4. Beat eggs and vanilla until foamy. Add sugar and beat until fluffy. Stir in chocolate-butter mixture. Fold in dry ingredients. Pour batter into five 8-ounce custard cups, filling nearly to rim. Place in baking pan; water should come halfway up sides of cups.
5. Bake for 30 minutes or until brownie tops are cracked and firm to the touch. Let cool for 5 minutes, then serve dusted with confectioners' sugar.

TOP: Braising with sugar and orange juice will slightly caramelize the fennel.
ABOVE: The butternut squash risotto is served in a Wedgwood White soup bowl, which is placed on a vintage Wedgwood plate.

2

LENTIL and
ESCAROLE SOUP

GRATIN of
YUKON GOLD POTATOES

LAMB CHOPS with
PRUNE CHUTNEY

PEARS GLAZED
with MAPLE SYRUP

PREPARATION SCHEDULE

1 Assemble gratin and begin
   baking.

2 Start soup.

3 Prepare chutney and croutons.

4. Whip cream and refrigerate.

5 Prepare lamb chops and
   finish soup.

6 Cook pears after dinner.

RIGHT: This yellow-potato gratin omits
the heavy cream yet keeps the rich flavor.
BELOW: A hand-blown Mexican tum-
bler is filled with sunflowers. Lamb
chops are topped with prune chutney.
BOTTOM LEFT: A small serving of
lentil-and-escarole soup is the perfect
start to this autumn meal.

LENTIL and ESCAROLE SOUP

serves 4

If you can't find French green lentils, substitute brown lentils.

1 tablespoon unsalted butter
½ medium onion, finely chopped
1 small clove garlic, finely chopped
1 small carrot, coarsely chopped
¾ cup French green lentils
1 bay leaf
2 whole canned tomatoes, drained, seeded, and coarsely chopped
1½ teaspoons salt
⅛ teaspoon freshly ground pepper
2 slices Italian bread, cut into ¾-inch cubes
½ head escarole, cut crosswise into 1-inch strips
2 teaspoons extra-virgin olive oil

1. In a stockpot, melt butter over medium heat. Add onion, garlic, and carrot; sauté until tender, about 5 minutes. Add lentils, bay leaf, tomatoes, salt, pepper, and 5½ cups water. Bring to a boil, reduce heat, and simmer until lentils are tender, about 40 minutes.
2. Meanwhile, heat oven to 425°. Toast the bread cubes on a baking sheet, turning them occasionally, until golden brown, about 7 minutes.
3. Add the escarole to the soup and cook for 5 minutes more. Adjust seasonings and serve soup in four bowls, topped with croutons and olive oil.

GRATIN of YUKON GOLD POTATOES

serves 4

Yellow Finn, or any other all-purpose medium-starch potato, can substitute for Yukon Gold.

½ tablespoon unsalted butter
6 Yukon Gold potatoes (about 1 pound)
⅔ cup grated Gruyère cheese (about 1½ ounces)
1 teaspoon olive oil
1 tablespoon fresh thyme leaves, plus 4 or 5 sprigs for garnish
¾ teaspoon salt
⅛ teaspoon freshly ground pepper
⅓ cup chicken stock, homemade or low-sodium canned

1. Heat oven to 400°. Butter a 9-inch round or oval baking dish.
2. Slice potatoes ⅛ inch thick and combine thoroughly in a mixing bowl with ⅓ cup of the Gruyère, the olive oil, thyme leaves, salt, and pepper.
3. Arrange potatoes in a neat overlapping pattern in the baking dish. Pour chicken stock over potatoes and sprinkle remaining cheese over top. Bake until potatoes are tender and the cheese and potatoes are starting to brown, about 45 minutes. Garnish with thyme sprigs.

LAMB CHOPS with PRUNE CHUTNEY

serves 4

If bite-size prunes are not available, larger prunes, cut into quarters, can be used instead.

1½ tablespoons unsalted butter
2 teaspoons sugar
8 shallots, peeled and cut in half lengthwise
1 tablespoon balsamic vinegar
½ cup chicken stock, homemade or low-sodium canned
2 tablespoons dried cranberries
18 bite-size prunes
1½ tablespoons chopped fresh rosemary, plus sprigs for garnish
Salt and freshly ground pepper
8 rib lamb chops, ¾ inch thick
1 tablespoon olive oil

1. Melt the butter in a skillet over medium heat. Add the sugar and shallots; cook until golden brown, about 15 minutes. Add the vinegar; cook until evaporated. Add the stock, fruit, 1 teaspoon of the chopped rosemary, and salt and pepper to taste. Cook until the shallots are tender and liquid is reduced by three-quarters, about 5 minutes. Keep warm.
2. Season lamb chops with salt, pepper, and remaining chopped rosemary. Heat olive oil in a skillet over medium heat. Add chops; sauté until brown on the bottom, 3 to 4 minutes. Turn and cook until a meat thermometer reads 110° (for medium rare) and chops are evenly browned, 3 to 4 minutes more. Garnish with rosemary sprigs and serve with the chutney.

Chutney is a classic Indian condiment that is made with fruit, vinegar, and sugar.

PEARS GLAZED
with MAPLE SYRUP

serves 4

When you buy pears, press gently on the stem end. A ripe pear will give slightly.

½   cup heavy cream
¼   teaspoon ground cardamom
3   Comice pears (about 1¾ pounds)
1   tablespoon lemon juice
1½   tablespoons unsalted butter
3   tablespoons pure maple syrup

1. In a chilled mixing bowl, combine the cream and the ground cardamom and whip until the cream holds soft peaks. Refrigerate, covered.

2. Quarter, core, and peel pears. Cut quarters in half and sprinkle with lemon juice.

3. Melt butter in a large skillet over medium-high heat. Arrange pears in skillet and cook on one side until pears just begin to brown, about 3 minutes. Add maple syrup and cook until pears are tender, about 1 minute more. Turn pears and cook for another minute. Remove from heat and allow pears to cool slightly. Transfer to bowls and serve warm, topped with whipped cream.

3

TOMATO and FRENCH BEAN SALAD

serves 4

Young, tender string beans may be substituted for the French beans.

1 tablespoon orange juice
1½ teaspoons lemon juice
1½ teaspoons reduced-sodium soy sauce
⅛ teaspoon ground coriander
½ teaspoon minced fresh ginger
½ teaspoon honey
1½ tablespoons vegetable oil
 Salt and freshly ground pepper
¼ pound French beans (haricots verts), stem ends removed and beans cut in half
3 ripe tomatoes (about 1½ pounds)
1 bunch arugula, stems removed and leaves cut in half

1. In a small bowl, combine orange and lemon juices, soy sauce, coriander, ginger, and honey. Whisk in oil and season to taste with salt and pepper.
2. Bring a pot of water to a boil. Add 1 teaspoon salt and the beans; cook until tender, about 2 minutes. Drain beans, then cool in ice water.
3. Slice tomatoes ¾ inch thick, and cut slices into chunks. Drain beans well and place in a bowl with tomatoes and arugula. Season with salt and pepper and toss with dressing. Arrange on four salad plates.

PREPARATION SCHEDULE

1 Prepare vegetables and fish, and start chowder.
2 Cook and cool blueberries for fool.
3 Prepare salad ingredients and make dressing.
4 Mix and bake biscuits. Finish chowder.
5 Prepare fool and chill in glasses.
6 Toss salad and serve with chowder and biscuits.

FISH CHOWDER

serves 4

Simmering the corncobs in the broth intensifies the flavor of this light chowder.

1 tablespoon unsalted butter
½ large yellow onion, peeled and finely chopped (about 1 cup)
2 ears corn, kernels cut off, cobs and kernels reserved
1 tablespoon chopped fresh oregano, plus sprigs for garnish
 Salt and freshly ground pepper
1 bay leaf
1¾ pounds small red potatoes, quartered
2 ounces each small yellow and green squash, sliced ¼ inch thick
½ red pepper, cut into ½-inch dice
1½ pounds firm white-fleshed fish fillets, such as red snapper or monkfish, cut into 1¼-inch pieces
½ cup milk

1. In a large saucepan, melt the butter over medium heat. Add the onion, corncobs, and oregano. Cook until the onions are translucent. Add 6 cups water, salt, pepper, and bay leaf. Bring to a simmer and add the potatoes. Cook, covered, until potatoes are tender, about 20 minutes.
2. Discard cobs. Remove half the potatoes and puree with 1 cup of the cooking liquid until smooth. Return puree to pan and stir.
3. Raise heat to medium. Add corn and remaining vegetables; cook until tender, about 5 minutes. Add fish; cook 5 minutes more, until fish is done. Stir in milk; adjust seasonings. Garnish with oregano sprigs.

OPPOSITE: This tomato-and-bean salad calls for arugula, a peppery Italian
green also known as rocket.
THIS PAGE: A light fish chowder is
served in deep-welled soup plates; the
spoon is coin silver.

Buttermilk makes these soda biscuits extra moist and flaky.

SODA BISCUITS

serves 4

Shaping the dough directly on the baking sheet makes short work of homemade biscuits.

1¾ cups all-purpose flour, sifted
1 teaspoon salt
1½ tablespoons sugar
1½ teaspoons baking soda
2 teaspoons baking powder
5 tablespoons cold unsalted butter, cut into small pieces
¾ cup buttermilk

1. Heat oven to 425°. Combine dry ingredients in the bowl of a food processor. Pulse once or twice to combine. Add butter and process until dough looks like coarse oatmeal. Add buttermilk and process again a few seconds more, until dough just comes together.
2. Turn out dough onto a parchment-lined baking sheet and pat into a 7-inch circle about 1 inch thick. Using a sharp knife, cut into 8 wedges, but do not separate.
3. Bake biscuits until golden brown on top and firm, about 20 to 25 minutes. Serve warm with butter.

BLUEBERRY FOOL

serves 4

A fool is a simple dessert made with fresh fruit and whipped cream.

½ pint fresh blueberries, washed and picked over
1 teaspoon lemon juice
1 tablespoon granulated sugar, or to taste
¾ cup heavy cream
2 tablespoons confectioners' sugar
1 teaspoon vanilla extract

1. In a small, nonreactive saucepan, combine blueberries, lemon juice, granulated sugar, and 2 tablespoons water. Cook over medium heat, stirring frequently, until blueberries begin to break down and juices boil and thicken, about 5 minutes. Remove from heat and transfer to a small bowl. Place bowl in a larger bowl of ice water and stir mixture occasionally until cold.
2. In a separate bowl, combine cream, confectioners' sugar, and vanilla. Beat until stiff peaks form; fold in ⅓ cup of the blueberry sauce. Divide among 4 dessert dishes and spoon remaining sauce over tops.

HOW TO BUY FISH

The first rule of fish buying is to select a fish that looks and smells fresh: With whole fish, the flesh should be firm and resilient to the touch, the eyes full and clear (the eye flattens and turns cloudy as the fish ages), and it should have a fresh, seaweedlike odor. With scaly fish, like salmon, the more scales that remain, the better the fish was handled.

Fillets should be shiny, free of any blood spots and bits of bone and skin, and should not curl at the edges or show signs of yellowing. They shouldn't be surrounded by liquid, a sign that they're old or have been improperly frozen. Fillets deteriorate more quickly than whole fish, so it's best to buy them at a market where they're filleted on the spot rather than sold precut. Although it's not possible to smell fish that is sold already wrapped, like whole fish it should bounce back when pressed.

Because most fish is flash-frozen on board the fishing boat, frozen fish is not necessarily a bad thing. In fact, if it has been properly frozen, it can taste better than fresh fish that is iced for days before it reaches the market.

A footed glass dessert cup, placed on an ironstone honey dish, holds dessert. Cream-soup spoons are ideal for scooping up the blueberry fool.

4

RAW ARTICHOKE and
MUSHROOM SALAD

EGGPLANT with
CHUNKY TOMATO SAUCE

PASTA WITH
CARAMELIZED ONIONS
and BITTER GREENS

MOCHA SHORTBREAD WEDGES

PREPARATION SCHEDULE

1 Make shortbread.

2 Make sauce for eggplant; keep warm.

3 Begin caramelizing onions.

4 Slice artichokes and mushrooms.

5 Cook eggplant.

6 Finish preparing pasta and salad.

RAW ARTICHOKE and MUSHROOM SALAD

serves 4

Four large artichokes can be used instead, but they should be completely trimmed, leaving only the hearts.

  3 lemons, halved
  6 baby artichokes (about 4 ounces each)
  6 cremini or white mushrooms
  3 tablespoons extra-virgin olive oil
     Salt and freshly ground pepper
  4 ounces Parmesan, thinly shaved

1. Squeeze lemons into a small bowl. Set aside. Pull off tough outer leaves from artichokes and discard. Trim bottoms and tops of artichokes. Slice lengthwise and pull out the fuzzy choke, if any. Slice artichokes crosswise as thinly as possible and immediately place in lemon juice to prevent browning.

2. Slice the mushrooms. Remove the artichokes from lemon juice with a slotted spoon, combine with mushrooms, and dress with olive oil, salt, and pepper. Toss with half of the Parmesan and arrange on 4 salad plates. Garnish with remaining cheese, and serve.

EGGPLANT with CHUNKY TOMATO SAUCE

serves 4

Simmering the eggplant in water removes the bitterness and allows it to be cooked with no added fat.

  6 plum tomatoes
1-2 cloves garlic, thinly sliced
  1 tablespoon olive oil
  1 tablespoon fresh thyme leaves, plus sprigs for garnish, or 1 teaspoon dried
     Salt and freshly ground pepper
  4 baby eggplants (3 to 4 ounces each)
  ½ cup ricotta, as garnish

1. Cut tomatoes into large chunks. In a large skillet over medium heat, sauté garlic in the olive oil until golden brown. Add tomatoes, thyme leaves, and salt and pepper to taste. Cook for 7 minutes, or until sauce is thick. Keep warm.

2. While sauce is cooking, prick eggplants in several places with a fork. Bring a saucepan of salted water to a boil and add eggplants. Cover and simmer 10 minutes, or until eggplants are tender.

3. Drain eggplants and place one on each of 4 plates. Slit open eggplants and spoon some tomato sauce inside each one. Garnish each plate with a spoonful of ricotta and a sprig of thyme.

PASTA with CARAMELIZED ONIONS and BITTER GREENS

serves 4

Use a regular skillet (not a nonstick pan) for this recipe; you'll get more flavor and color in the sauce.

1 tablespoon olive oil
1-2 tablespoons unsalted butter
4 medium onions, peeled and cut into ¼-inch-thick rings
1 teaspoon sugar
4 cups chicken broth (preferably homemade) or water
   Salt and freshly ground pepper
1 pound fettuccine
1 head chicory (curly endive), mustard greens, kale, or arugula, washed, with tough ribs removed and leaves torn into pieces

1. Heat oil and 1 tablespoon butter in a large, heavy skillet over medium-high heat. Add onions and sugar and cook, stirring once or twice, until well browned, about 10 minutes. Turn heat to low; continue to cook, stirring occasionally, until very soft, about 10 minutes.

2. Remove half the onions and set aside. Add broth or water to the pan and bring to a boil. Cook over high heat, scraping bottom of pan, for 10 minutes. Season to taste with salt and pepper.

3. Cook the pasta in boiling salted water until a little underdone, and drain. Add to the broth and simmer for 2 to 3 minutes. Add greens and cook, covered, until wilted, about 1 minute. Stir in additional tablespoon of butter, if desired. Divide among four shallow bowls, garnish with reserved onions, and serve.

LEFT: An English ironstone dinner plate is deep enough to contain the juices from the pasta sauce.

BELOW: The addition of ground espresso beans intensifies the flavor of these shortbread wedges. The coffee is served in a faceted vintage chocolate cup.

MOCHA SHORTBREAD WEDGES

serves 4 to 6

This not-too-sweet shortbread can also be rolled out and cut, but baking it in a pan and cutting while warm is faster and easier.

11 tablespoons (½ cup plus 3 tablespoons) all-purpose flour
½ cup unsweetened cocoa powder
   Pinch of salt
1 tablespoon finely ground coffee beans, preferably espresso
8 tablespoons (1 stick) unsalted butter, softened
⅓ cup confectioners' sugar, plus more for sprinkling

1. Heat oven to 350°. Sift together flour, cocoa, and salt. Stir in coffee and set aside.

2. Beat butter until smooth. Add sugar and beat well. Add flour mixture and beat until combined.

3. Pat dough into an ungreased 8-inch round pan. Bake for 20 to 25 minutes, or until firm. Remove shortbread from oven and let sit for 5 minutes, then cut into wedges. Let cool completely. Sprinkle with confectioners' sugar before serving.

FOUR BEET SALAD
on ARUGULA with SHERRY
VINAIGRETTE

MEDALLIONS of PORK
with SOUR CHERRY SAUCE

HERBED MASHED POTATOES

CORNMEAL FRIED
TOMATOES

APPLE PHYLLO
CORNUCOPIAS

PREPARATION SCHEDULE

1 Prepare apple mixture; chill.

2 Bake beets and let steam;
   cook dried cherries with port
   and let soak.

3 Simmer potatoes and infuse
   cream-herb mixture.

4 Prepare vinaigrette; prepare
   apple phyllo cornucopias and
   set aside, unbaked.

5 Prepare fried tomatoes.

6 Sauté pork and finish cherry
   sauce; finish preparing mashed
   potatoes.

7 Just before serving dinner,
   place cornucopias in oven.

FOUR BEET SALAD on ARUGULA with SHERRY VINAIGRETTE

serves 4

*The sweet beets and bitter greens
make a wonderful contrast of flavors and
colors. We used orange, red, yellow,
and white beets.*

1 pound beets
½ teaspoon grainy mustard
2 tablespoons sherry vinegar
   Pinch of sugar
6 tablespoons extra-virgin olive oil
   Salt and freshly ground pepper
1 large bunch arugula

1. Heat oven to 400°. Wash the beets and
cut stalks to ½ inch. Reserve beet greens, if
any (see Note). Place the beets on a sheet
of aluminum foil and form a pouch, seal-
ing tightly. Place on a baking sheet and
bake for 35 minutes.
2. Remove the beets from the oven and allow them to steam in the pouch for 10 minutes longer. Take the beets out of the
pouch and place in the refrigerator. When
cool, slip the beets out of their skins and
slice. Set aside.
3. To make the vinaigrette, whisk together
mustard, vinegar, and sugar in a small
bowl. Slowly whisk in the oil, and season
with salt and pepper.
4. Toss the beets with the vinaigrette and
serve on a bed of arugula.
NOTE: *For a delicious alternative to the
usual leafy vegetables, place washed beet
greens in a pot with a little olive oil and
some minced garlic. Cover and turn up
heat to medium. Cook until just wilted.*

MEDALLIONS of PORK with SOUR CHERRY SAUCE

serves 4

*Dried sour cherries add a sweet-tart taste
to the sauce; they are available at
specialty-food stores.*

2 pounds pork-loin roast,
   trimmed of fat
1 cup dried sour cherries
1 cup port wine
1 teaspoon unsalted butter
1 teaspoon olive oil
   Salt and freshly ground pepper
¼ cup balsamic vinegar

1. Cut pork into ¼-inch slices. Place between 2 sheets of plastic wrap and pound
thin with a mallet or the side of a cleaver.
2. In a small saucepan over medium heat,
combine the dried sour cherries with ⅓
cup of the port. Bring to a simmer, then
turn off heat. Let the cherries soak until
you need them.
3. In a medium sauté pan (not nonstick)
over medium-high heat, cook butter with
olive oil until light brown. Cook the pork
slices in 2 batches, allowing them to brown
well around the edges, about 1 to 2 minutes on each side. Transfer slices to a warm
plate and sprinkle with salt and pepper. Do
not allow pan drippings to burn.
4. Remove pan from heat. Add the balsamic vinegar, scraping the pan with a
wooden spoon. Return pan to heat and
add the remaining ⅔ cup wine. Boil over
high heat until thick, about 1 minute. Combine with the cherries and spoon over
meat. Serve immediately.

LEFT: Comfort food is best eaten in a comfortable setting—a faded cotton tablecloth, drabware plates, Bakelite-handled flatware, and amethyst Depression glasses. An urn filled with apples serves as a centerpiece.

BELOW: Mellow-tasting sherry vinegar goes well with the sweet beets and peppery arugula.

ABOVE: Beet greens can be prepared like any other greens and have even more nutrients than beet roots. They're served with tomatoes fried in yellow cornmeal and herbed mashed potatoes.

HERBED MASHED POTATOES

serves 4

Almost any combination of fresh herbs can be used.

6 large white potatoes, peeled and cut into medium chunks
  Pinch of salt
1 cup heavy cream or milk
1 tablespoon chopped fresh sage
1 tablespoon chopped rosemary
1 tablespoon chopped thyme
4 tablespoons (½ stick) unsalted butter, cut into pieces
1 tablespoon chopped fresh parsley
  Freshly ground pepper

CORNMEAL FRIED TOMATOES

serves 4

This is a good use for extra tomatoes. Green tomatoes are also delicious prepared this way.

Olive oil
2 large or 3 small tomatoes
  Yellow cornmeal
  Salt and freshly ground pepper

Heat a small quantity of oil in a sauté pan over medium-high heat. Cut tomatoes into ¼-inch slices. Dredge in cornmeal, coating well on both sides. Fry until golden brown, turning once, and drain on paper towels. Season to taste with salt and pepper.

1. Place potato chunks in a large saucepan over high heat and cover with cold water. Add salt and bring to a boil. Lower heat and simmer until potatoes are tender, about 20 minutes.

2. In a small saucepan over medium heat, combine cream or milk and all the herbs except parsley. Bring to a simmer, then turn off heat and cover, allowing herbs to infuse for 15 minutes.

3. Drain potatoes well and pass through a food mill (or use a masher). Add butter and gradually stir in cream or milk until potatoes have desired consistency (you may not need all the cream or milk). Stir in parsley, season with additional salt and pepper, and serve.

APPLE PHYLLO CORNUCOPIAS
serves 4

Phyllo dough can be found in the freezer section at most supermarkets. The apple mixture can be made ahead of time and refrigerated until ready to use.

6 Granny Smith apples
1 tablespoon unsalted butter
½ cup sugar
1 teaspoon cinnamon
½ teaspoon ground ginger
¼ teaspoon ground cloves
Dash of vanilla extract
Juice of ½ lemon
1 box phyllo dough, thawed according to package directions
Walnut oil or melted butter
Vanilla ice cream

1. Peel and core the apples and cut them into small chunks.

2. In a small saucepan over medium heat, melt butter. Add apples, sugar, spices, vanilla, and lemon juice, and cook until apples are soft but still firm, about 10 minutes. Spread on a plate and refrigerate.

3. Heat oven to 400°. Unroll phyllo dough and cover with a damp towel. Remove 4 sheets from pile (do not separate) and brush top with walnut oil or butter. Cut into thirds lengthwise. Remove 4 more sheets, cut one strip the same size as the others, and brush with oil or butter. (Wrap remaining dough in plastic; refrigerate or freeze for later use.)

4. Spoon the apple mixture onto ends of strips. Roll into free-form cone shapes, loosely gathering and folding back the excess dough. Place the cones on a baking sheet seam side down and bake for 30 minutes or until golden brown. Serve with vanilla ice cream.

RIGHT: The apple phyllo cornucopia is served on an amber pressed-glass plate with an antique silver fork.

6

WARM POTATO and
WATERCRESS SALAD

ROASTED CORN
with OREGANO BUTTER

EGGPLANT and
LAMB AL FORNO

TAPIOCA PUDDING
with SAUTÉED NECTARINES

PREPARATION SCHEDULE

1 Make pudding.

2 Salt eggplant, make sauce,
   assemble layers, and bake.

3 Roast potatoes; make
   vinaigrette.

4 Prepare and roast corn.

5 Toss potato salad.

6 After dinner, sauté nectarines.

LEFT: Sprigs of oregano are placed on ears of corn, which are then baked in the husk.
BELOW: Warm red potatoes and watercress are served in a nineteenth-century American milk pan.

WARM POTATO and WATERCRESS SALAD

serves 4

Warm potatoes and cool greens are a perfect combination for a late-summer meal.

- 12 small red potatoes (about 1 pound 6 ounces), scrubbed
- 3 tablespoons olive oil
- 1 teaspoon salt
- ½ teaspoon freshly ground pepper
- 2 teaspoons fresh lemon juice
- 1 teaspoon sherry vinegar
- 1 bunch watercress (about 6 ounces), tough stems removed
  Zest of half a lemon

1. Heat oven to 375°. Arrange potatoes in a roasting pan and add 1 tablespoon olive oil, ½ teaspoon salt, and ¼ teaspoon pepper; roll potatoes to coat. Roast until potatoes are tender, about 40 minutes. Remove from oven and let stand just until cool enough to handle.

2. Meanwhile, whisk together lemon juice, vinegar, remaining 2 tablespoons olive oil, and remaining ½ teaspoon salt and ¼ teaspoon pepper in a medium bowl; set aside.

3. Break each warm potato in half and place in a serving bowl. Add the vinaigrette and toss to coat. Add watercress and lemon zest, toss, and serve immediately.

ROASTED CORN with OREGANO BUTTER

serves 4

Sprigs of herbs tucked inside the husk lend their fresh flavor to the corn.

- 4 tablespoons unsalted butter, softened
- ½ cup fresh oregano leaves, plus 8 sprigs
- 1 teaspoon salt
- ½ teaspoon freshly ground pepper
- 4 ears corn (about 2½ pounds)

1. Heat oven to 375. Place butter on a cutting board and sprinkle with oregano leaves, ½ teaspoon salt, and ¼ teaspoon pepper. Chop with a sharp knife until butter is smooth and the oregano and seasonings are fully incorporated. Transfer to a small dish and set aside.

2. Trim stems and discard tough outer husks from corncobs. Peel back remaining husks, being careful not to detach them from the corn. Discard corn silk.

3. Use a pastry brush to spread the herb butter evenly over the kernels and season with remaining ½ teaspoon salt and ¼ teaspoon pepper. Place 2 sprigs of oregano on each ear of corn and pull husks back up to enclose corn and herbs. Wrap kitchen string around the tip of the ear and tie.

4. Place corn on a baking sheet and roast, turning once, until corn is fragrant and tender, about 25 minutes. Remove string. Pull back the husks and tie them in a knot, if desired. Season to taste and serve.

Corn, which has been cultivated for more than seven thousand years, is both a grain and a vegetable. It can be eaten at every stage of its growing season, from when the ear is a few tender inches long to when the kernels are old and dry. Yet the sweet-corn season lasts for only a short time, from late June to the beginning of October, depending on the region.

The key to sweet corn is freshness. Ideally, corn should be eaten as soon as possible after picking, before its sugars convert to starch. Be sure to choose ears whose husks and silk are moist, not dried out. Kernel color is a matter of personal taste: Bicolored sweet corn is preferred in the Northeast and West. White is the color of choice in the South, yellow in the Midwest.

Preparing fresh corn is simple: It needs no more than two minutes in boiling water; the youngest, sweetest ears may need only a few seconds. (Don't add salt to the water, since it toughens the kernels.) Sweet corn is best eaten plain, but adding flavorings such as fresh herbs, chili powder, cayenne pepper, garlic, or lime juice to melted butter enhances the corn's natural flavors.

EGGPLANT and LAMB AL FORNO

serves 4

Salting eggplant allows it to release any bitter juices.

Salt and freshly ground black pepper
2   medium eggplants (about 1½ pounds total), ends trimmed, cut into six ¼-inch-thick rounds each
1   tablespoon olive oil
1   medium onion, cut into ¼-inch dice
1   teaspoon each dried oregano, cinnamon, and ground cumin
¼   teaspoon cayenne pepper
1¼ pounds ground lamb
1   28-ounce can whole, peeled plum tomatoes, drained
2   teaspoons coarsely chopped flat-leaf parsley
1   tablespoon dry bread crumbs

1. Heat oven to 375°. Salt eggplant well, arrange in colanders, and place weighted bowls on top; let drain for 30 minutes. Rinse and dry.
2. Heat oil in a large skillet over medium heat. Add onion, 1 teaspoon salt, and ¾ teaspoon black pepper; cook until tender, 7 to 10 minutes. Add oregano, cinnamon, cumin, and cayenne; cook for 2 minutes more. Add lamb and cook until it browns, about 5 minutes. Drain fat from pan. Break up tomatoes and add to pan. Cook over medium heat, stirring often, until sauce starts to thicken, about 8 minutes.
3. Place four eggplant slices in an 8-inch square baking pan and top with a third of the sauce. Repeat twice, making four 3-layer stacks. Combine 1 teaspoon parsley and bread crumbs; sprinkle over the top.
4. Cover with foil and bake for 1 hour. Remove foil and bake for 10 to 15 minutes more. Sprinkle with remaining parsley; serve.

Cumin and cinnamon give this lamb—in a square Wedgwood dish—an exotic sweet flavor.

TAPIOCA PUDDING WITH SAUTÉED NECTARINES

serves 4

Warm nectarines update this childhood favorite.

3   tablespoons quick-cooking tapioca
¼   cup sugar
¼   cup honey
¼   teaspoon salt
2   large eggs
2   cups milk
2   large nectarines (about 10 ounces total), each sliced into 10 wedges
¼   teaspoon ground ginger
4   sprigs mint (optional)

1. Combine tapioca, sugar, 2 tablespoons honey, salt, eggs, and milk in a medium saucepan and whisk to combine. Let stand, without stirring, for about 5 minutes. Cook over medium heat, stirring, until mixture comes to a full boil.
2. Transfer tapioca mixture to a medium bowl set over a bowl of ice water. Let stand to cool, stirring occasionally, 12 to 15 minutes. When cool, pudding can be refrigerated for up to 1 day before serving.
3. Meanwhile, heat the remaining 2 tablespoons honey in a medium skillet over medium heat. Add the nectarine wedges and sprinkle with ginger. Cook until the fruit is just tender, 2 to 3 minutes. Divide the pudding among four dishes and spoon the nectarines over. Top each with a sprig of mint, if desired.

WARM PEAR SALAD

serves 4

*Sautéed pears make this salad
a satisfying start to an autumn meal.*

2   Bartlett pears, ripe but firm
5   teaspoons olive oil
1   teaspoon honey
½   teaspoon dry mustard
½   teaspoon salt
⅛   teaspoon freshly ground pepper
½   medium red onion, thinly sliced
     into rings
2   heads endive, sliced crosswise
     into 1-inch pieces
1   bunch watercress, tough
     stems removed
¼   pound Stilton or Roquefort cheese,
     crumbled
1½ teaspoons red-wine vinegar
1   teaspoon Worcestershire sauce

1. Cut pears lengthwise into quarters. Peel, core, and cut each quarter into approximately 1-inch chunks and place in a small bowl. Add 2 teaspoons olive oil, honey, dry mustard, salt, and pepper and toss well.
2. Place a medium skillet over medium-high heat. Add pears and onions and cook, shaking the skillet a few times, until pears are golden brown and onions are slightly wilted, about 3 minutes.
3. Transfer pears, onions, and any juices to a bowl. Add endive, watercress, cheese, remaining olive oil, vinegar, and Worcestershire sauce and toss together gently. Season to taste with salt and pepper; serve warm.

7

WARM PEAR SALAD

CORNISH HENS
with KASHA PILAF

CARROT and
PARSNIP PUREE

CHOCOLATE KISSES

PREPARATION SCHEDULE

1. Prepare cookie batter and bake. Cook pasta.
2. Cook carrots and parsnips; keep warm.
3. Start onions and mushrooms; add the kasha.
4. Melt chocolate, fill kisses, and let harden.
5. Cook Cornish hens. Make puree; keep warm.
6. Prepare ingredients for salad and sauté pears.
7. Make sauce for hens; combine kasha and pasta.
8. Toss salad and remove hens from oven.

CORNISH HENS with KASHA PILAF

serves 4

*Kasha is buckwheat, and can be found
in the grains section of the supermarket or
health-food store.*

4   tablespoons butter
1   medium onion, cut into ¼-inch dice
½   pound white mushrooms,
     stemmed and quartered
½   cup whole kasha
2½ cups homemade or low-sodium
     canned chicken stock
     Flour, seasoned with salt and
     pepper, for dredging
2   two-pound Cornish hens, split,
     with backbones reserved
¼   cup white wine
½   pound orecchiette pasta,
     cooked al dente
⅓   cup loosely packed parsley leaves,
     finely chopped

1. Heat oven to 425°; place a roasting pan in it. Melt 2 tablespoons butter in a skillet over medium heat. Add onions, cook 10 to 12 minutes, then add mushrooms and cook until tender. Add kasha and 2 cups stock. Cook until kasha is tender, about 20 minutes. Set aside.
2. Melt 1½ tablespoons butter in a cast-iron skillet over medium-high heat. Flour hens and cook, skin side down, with backbones, until brown, 6 to 8 minutes. Turn and cook 3 to 5 more minutes. Transfer hens to roasting pan; roast for about 20 minutes.
3. Pour grease from skillet. Over high heat, add wine and use a wooden spoon to scrape up brown bits. Lower heat, add remaining stock, and cook until reduced by a third, 5 minutes. Stir in remaining butter.
4. Stir cooked pasta and parsley into kasha. Season and heat through.
5. Serve hens over kasha pilaf and spoon sauce over hens.

The Cornish hens and kasha pilaf are brought to the table on a fish platter, then served on handmade stoneware plates with the carrot and parsnip puree. The kasha is mixed with ear-shaped pasta in a variation on kasha varnishkes, a traditional Jewish dish.

LEFT: Purees are a delicious way of combining root vegetables such as the carrots and parsnips used here.

CARROT and PARSNIP PUREE

serves 4

Parsnips, an often overlooked vegetable, lend their sweet and spicy flavor to this creamy puree.

6   medium carrots (about 1 pound)
3   medium parsnips (about 14 ounces)
1   tablespoon salt
2   large cloves garlic, peeled
4   sprigs fresh thyme, plus 1 tablespoon leaves, plus more for garnish
2   tablespoons butter
1   tablespoon heavy cream
    Freshly ground pepper

1. Peel the carrots and parsnips and cut into approximately 2-inch chunks. Fill a medium saucepan with 6 cups cold water, bring to a boil, and add salt. Place carrots, garlic, and 4 sprigs of thyme in the water, reduce heat, and simmer for about 5 minutes. Add parsnips and continue cooking until both carrots and parsnips are soft, about 15 minutes.

2. Remove from heat, drain, and discard thyme sprigs. Transfer carrots, parsnips, and garlic to the work bowl of a food processor. Add butter, cream, and 1 tablespoon thyme leaves and process until completely smooth. Season to taste with salt and pepper. Serve immediately, garnished with fresh thyme, if desired. This can be made ahead of time and warmed in a saucepan over low heat to serve.

CHOCOLATE KISSES

makes 16

These chewy macaroons call for two favorite flavors, chocolate and almonds.

2   large egg whites
1   cup sugar
6   tablespoons cocoa, sifted
1½ cups medium-fine ground blanched almonds (about 6¼ ounces)
½   teaspoon shortening
4   ounces semisweet chocolate, melted

1. Heat oven to 325°. Place egg whites in the clean bowl of an electric mixer. Beat on high speed, using the whisk attachment, until egg whites are stiff. Then add the sugar slowly and continue beating until egg whites are very thick, about 2 to 3 minutes.

2. Beat in cocoa until combined. Stir in almonds and mix until completely blended. The batter should be quite thick and sticky.

3. Line a baking sheet with parchment. Dampen your hands and shape about 1 heaping teaspoonful of dough into a 1-inch ball. Pinch the ball with your fingers to form a teardrop shape and place on prepared baking sheet. Continue the process, spacing cookies about 2 inches apart, until all the dough is used.

4. Bake until cookies are slightly cracked, 15 to 17 minutes. Let cool on sheet for several minutes, then transfer cookies to a rack to cool completely.

5. Combine shortening and melted chocolate. Spoon about ½ teaspoon of the chocolate onto the flat side of a cooled cookie and place another cookie on top. Press together gently so the chocolate oozes out slightly. Return cookie to rack and let chocolate harden. Repeat the process with remaining cookies.

An antique ironstone butter chip is just
the right size for a chocolate kiss.

8

MIXED CHICORY
with HONEY VINAIGRETTE

HERBED GARLIC BREAD

PENNE with
TOMATOES and PANCETTA

FIG and
HAZELNUT TARTS

PREPARATION SCHEDULE

1 Assemble and bake tart.

2 Prepare pasta sauce.

3 Mix herbs and oil, spread on bread, and warm in oven.

4 Cook pasta and whisk together vinaigrette.

5 Toss pasta with sauce, dress salad, and serve dinner.

MIXED CHICORY
with HONEY VINAIGRETTE

serves 4

This sweet vinaigrette contrasts perfectly with the bitter greens.

1½ tablespoons fresh lemon juice
1½ teaspoons sherry vinegar
1 tablespoon honey
4½ tablespoons extra-virgin olive oil
1 teaspoon salt, plus more to taste
½ teaspoon freshly ground pepper, plus more to taste
1 teaspoon aniseed
1 small head escarole (about 8 ounces)
1 head radicchio (about 6 ounces)
1 small red onion (about 4 ounces), thinly sliced
1 fennel bulb (about 9 ounces), trimmed and cut into ½-inch-square pieces

1. Combine lemon juice, vinegar, and honey in a small bowl. Whisk in olive oil, salt, pepper, and aniseed. Set aside.

2. Remove tough outer leaves from escarole and radicchio and discard. Slice escarole into ¼-inch strips. Tear radicchio into bite-size pieces. Combine escarole, radicchio, red onion, and fennel in serving bowl; add vinaigrette and toss well. Adjust seasoning to taste with additional salt and pepper, if necessary, and serve.

PENNE with
TOMATOES and PANCETTA

serves 4

Pancetta is Italian bacon; if you can't find it, regular bacon can be substituted.

¼ cup olive oil
¼ pound pancetta, cut into ¼-inch cubes
1 onion (about ½ pound), peeled and cut into ½-inch dice
2 small cloves garlic, minced
Salt and freshly ground pepper
2 28-ounce cans plum tomatoes, drained, juice reserved
4 carrots, peeled and cut into ½-inch pieces
1 28-ounce can white kidney or cannellini beans, drained and rinsed
2 tablespoons coarsely chopped fresh sage leaves, plus 8 whole leaves
1 pound penne pasta
¼ cup shaved Parmesan

1. Heat 1 tablespoon oil in a large heavy saucepan over medium heat. Add pancetta; cook, stirring often, until golden brown, about 10 minutes. Add onions, garlic, ½ teaspoon salt, and ¼ teaspoon pepper. Cook, stirring often, until onions are golden, 7 to 10 minutes.

2. Seed tomatoes and cut into ½-inch pieces. Add reserved tomato juice and carrots to the pan. Cook until carrots are tender, about 10 minutes. Reduce heat to medium low, add tomatoes, beans, and chopped sage. Simmer until heated through, about 5 minutes.

3. Bring a pot of water to a boil; add 1½ teaspoons salt and pasta; cook until al dente. Meanwhile, heat remaining 3 tablespoons oil in a small skillet over medium heat. Fry sage leaves until they begin to curl. Blot on paper towels. Drain pasta and transfer to a serving bowl.

4. Add sauce; toss to combine. Serve with fried sage and Parmesan.

RIGHT: A 1950s yellow compote makes an unusual serving dish for the mixed-chicory salad.

OPPOSITE: The natural tones of this table setting—a white, wave-patterned plate and an unbleached linen tablecloth and dish towel (used as a napkin)—emphasize the brightly colored penne.

The tarts are made with black Mission figs, which are sweeter than the green-skinned variety.

LEFT: Pans with removable bottoms make it easier to loosen the fig and hazelnut tarts.
BELOW: This garlic bread is brushed with olive oil, lemon juice, and herbs instead of the usual butter.

FIG and HAZELNUT TARTS

serves 4

If you can't find skinned hazelnuts in a specialty store, substitute blanched almonds.

- 8 fresh figs, preferably black Mission
- 1½ cups skinned hazelnuts (6 ounces), toasted
- 2 tablespoons all-purpose flour
- ½ cup plus 1 tablespoon confectioners' sugar
- 1 large egg plus 1 large egg white
- 2 tablespoons unsalted butter, melted and cooled
- 1 tablespoon brandy
- ⅛ teaspoon freshly ground pepper
- 2 teaspoons grated lemon zest
  Nonstick vegetable-oil spray

1. Heat oven to 375°. Cut 6 figs into ¾-inch dice. Set aside in a bowl.

2. In a food processor, process nuts until medium fine. Sift together flour and ½ cup confectioners' sugar; add to nuts; pulse to combine. Add egg white, egg, butter, brandy, pepper, and zest. Process to combine, about 10 seconds. Add batter to figs and mix together.

3. Spray four 3¾-inch (or one 8-inch) tart pans with vegetable-oil spray. Divide the batter evenly among the pans. Cut remaining 2 figs lengthwise into 6 slices each. Arrange 3 slices over each tart. Place the tart pans on a baking sheet. Bake until tarts are set and golden brown, about 40 minutes (for individual tarts or 1 large tart). Remove from oven and cool slightly. Remove the tarts from the pans, sprinkle with remaining sugar, and serve.

HERBED GARLIC BREAD

serves 4

Different fresh or dried herbs can be used to suit your taste or the time of year.

- ½ cup loosely packed flat-leaf parsley leaves, coarsely chopped
- ½ teaspoon dried thyme
- 1 teaspoon fresh lemon juice
- 2 medium cloves garlic, minced
- ½ teaspoon salt
- ¼ teaspoon freshly ground pepper
- ¼ cup olive oil
- 1 12-inch-long loaf Italian-style white bread

1. Heat oven to 350°. Whisk together parsley, thyme, lemon juice, garlic, salt, pepper, and olive oil in a small bowl.

2. Using a bread knife, slice loaf into 12 half-inch pieces, cutting only three-quarters of the way through the loaf so it stays intact. Brush the herb mixture liberally between each slice. Wrap the loaf loosely in foil. Heat until warm, about 10 minutes. Serve immediately.

winter

Winter food tends to be hearty—stews, casseroles, roasts—and somewhat time-consuming. But that doesn't mean dinner has to be heavy or difficult to prepare. The simple recipes in this chapter are every bit as comforting as their more filling counterparts. They're perfect cold-weather dishes, whether you're planning a casual fireside meal with friends or an intimate dinner for two.

Since the selection of fruits and vegetables is more limited than at other times of year, the recipes combine them in unexpected ways. A salad of frisée, Belgian endive, and fennel is sprinkled with toasted hazelnuts. Sweet roasted beets are flavored with fresh grated ginger, and Granny Smith apples and leeks are sautéed together in a simple side dish. Most of the main courses highlight meat and seafood—sausage with stewed red onions uses veal in place of the more traditional pork, and sea scallops are served in a flavorful herb broth—but there is also a meatless menu featuring a potato-and-greens soup and red-cabbage-and-onion tarts. As for dessert, it couldn't be easier: Pineapple, sautéed with dark-brown sugar and vanilla, is served with ice cream; a square of semisweet chocolate is tucked into puff pastry and baked.

1

WHITE BEAN and
MUSHROOM RAGOUT

SEA SCALLOPS in HERB BROTH

WINTER SPINACH SALAD

ALMOND CAKE with
CARAMELIZED ORANGES

PREPARATION SCHEDULE

1 Make almond cake.

2 Start herb broth.

3 Wash spinach and prepare
   ingredients for salad and
   ragout.

4 Start ragout; sear scallops
   and keep warm.

5 Toss salad and finish herb
   broth.

6 Caramelize oranges.

BELOW LEFT: Chanterelles are best in simple dishes like this bean ragout, since their flavor is obscured by complex seasonings. The bowl is French restaurant ware.

LEFT: If the sea scallops are very large, cut them in half horizontally before cooking.

WHITE BEAN and
MUSHROOM RAGOUT

serves 4

*This ragout is meant to be a
side dish, but it can be served with a
green salad for a light lunch.*

½ pound assorted wild mushrooms,
   such as chanterelles and cremini

1 tablespoon olive oil

2 cloves garlic, peeled and thinly sliced
   Salt and freshly ground pepper

½ cup white wine

1 16-ounce can cannellini beans,
   drained and rinsed

¼ cup water

1. Carefully brush the mushrooms with a
mushroom brush or towel to remove any
dirt. Cut the larger mushrooms in half or
into ½-inch slices; keep the smaller mushrooms whole.

2. In a large skillet, heat the olive oil over
medium heat. Add the mushrooms, garlic,
and salt and pepper to taste. Cook for 3
minutes, until the mushrooms are lightly
browned. Add wine, beans, and water;
cook for 3 minutes more, until the mushrooms are soft and beans are heated
through. Adjust seasonings and keep warm
until ready to serve.

SEA SCALLOPS in HERB BROTH

serves 4

*The parsley and watercress turn this
broth a vibrant green.*

1 bunch flat-leaf parsley (about 2 cups)

1 bunch watercress (about 1½ cups),
   tough stems removed

2 shallots, coarsely chopped

1½ cups water

1 teaspoon salt, plus more for scallops

16 sea scallops (about 1 pound)
   Freshly ground pepper

1 teaspoon olive oil

1 teaspoon unsalted butter

1. In a medium saucepan, combine 1½
cups parsley, 1 cup watercress, shallots, water, and 1 teaspoon salt. Bring to a boil. Reduce heat; cover and simmer for 30
minutes. Strain; reserve liquid. Set aside.

2. Season scallops on both sides with salt
and pepper. Heat ½ teaspoon oil and ½
teaspoon butter in a large skillet over medium heat. Cook half the scallops for 5 minutes, or until golden brown. Turn and
cook for 3 more minutes. Keep warm; repeat process.

3. Return broth to a boil. In a blender,
combine remaining parsley and watercress
with hot broth. Cover blender with a towel
to absorb any splashes, hold top firmly in
place, and puree. Strain, and adjust seasonings. Pour broth into serving dish; place
scallops on top.

Seared sea scallops in a parsley-and-watercress broth make a light winter supper. Serve the white bean and wild mushroom ragout in the broth, as shown here, or on a separate plate.

WINTER SPINACH SALAD

serves 4

Currants or dried apricots can be substituted for the dried sour cherries.

1 bunch spinach, preferably flat-leaf, roughly chopped (about 6 cups)
⅓ cup dried sour cherries
3 scallions, thinly sliced
1 green apple, cored and thinly sliced
½ cup seedless red grapes, cut in half
¼ cup walnuts, coarsely chopped
2 teaspoons apple-cider vinegar
2 tablespoons olive oil
 Salt and freshly ground pepper
⅓ cup (about 2 ounces) crumbled goat cheese

Combine the spinach, cherries, scallions, apple slices, grapes, and walnuts. Whisk together vinegar and olive oil, and season to taste with salt and pepper. Pour the vinaigrette over the salad, toss in cheese, and arrange on salad plates.

ALMOND CAKE with CARAMELIZED ORANGES

serves 8

The cake keeps well for several days, wrapped in plastic.

10 tablespoons (1 stick plus 2 tablespoons) unsalted butter
2 cups sugar
1½ cups cake flour, sifted
2 tablespoons heavy cream
 Pinch of salt
3 large eggs, at room temperature
1 teaspoon almond extract
 Grated zest of 1 orange
4 navel oranges

1. Heat oven to 325°. Butter and flour an 8-inch round cake pan. In a large bowl, beat butter and 1½ cups sugar until fluffy. Add flour, alternating with cream, in two additions. Add salt. Beat in eggs one at a time. Stir in almond extract and orange zest. Bake for 1 hour, or until golden brown and a toothpick inserted in the center comes out clean.

2. Meanwhile, peel 3 oranges with a sharp knife, removing all of the white pith, and cut crosswise into ½-inch-thick rounds. Cut largest rounds in half. Squeeze juice from fourth orange into a heavy-bottomed skillet; add remaining ½ cup sugar. Cook over medium heat until golden-brown caramel forms, about 5 minutes. Add orange rounds and cook until glazed, 1 to 2 minutes. Serve at once with cake.

2

WINTER WHITE SALAD

PEPPERED STEAK SANDWICHES

CARAMELIZED SHALLOTS

BANANAS in BROWN
SUGAR and RUM

PREPARATION SCHEDULE

1 Trim steaks, coat with pepper, and refrigerate.

2 Cut vegetables for salad, toast hazelnuts, and prepare vinaigrette.

3 Caramelize shallots; set aside.

4 Prepare toasted baguette slices for sandwiches.

5 Cook steaks and let rest.

6 Finish salad.

7 Slice steak; prepare sandwiches.

8 Serve dinner.

9 Sauté bananas; serve dessert.

ABOVE: A nineteenth-century English ironstone plate and bowl hold the steak sandwich and the winter white salad. The flatware is French hotel silver and the celadon-bordered napkin is linen.

ABOVE RIGHT: Bananas are sautéed in brown sugar and rum and served on a ruffle-patterned plate.

RIGHT: Purple-hued shallots taste like a combination of onion and garlic.

WINTER WHITE SALAD

serves 4

Hazelnut oil has a subtle, nutty flavor that is perfect with winter vegetables. You can also use walnut oil or extra-virgin olive oil.

- 1 small head frisée or escarole
- 2 large heads Belgian endive
- 1 bulb fennel
- 1 leek, split lengthwise and thoroughly washed
- 1 stalk celery
- ½ cup whole hazelnuts
- 2 tablespoons white-wine vinegar
- ½ teaspoon Dijon mustard
- Salt and freshly ground pepper
- 6 tablespoons hazelnut oil

1. Tear frisée into medium pieces. Separate endive leaves. Quarter fennel bulb and slice as thinly as possible, using a mandoline or vegetable slicer. Slice one half of leek thinly crosswise, reserving other half for another use. Peel celery and slice paper thin on the diagonal. Refrigerate vegetables in covered bowls until ready to use.
2. Toast hazelnuts at 350° until skins blister and they give off a nutty aroma. Wrap in a clean kitchen towel and, when cool enough to handle, rub off skins. Set aside to cool completely.
3. Whisk together vinegar, mustard, and salt and pepper to taste. Slowly add the oil.
4. Toss each vegetable separately with a little dressing, and arrange on cold plates. Crush the hazelnuts lightly with the back of a knife and sprinkle some over each salad. Serve immediately.

PEPPERED STEAK SANDWICHES

serves 4

You can use a less expensive steak than we've suggested, such as London broil—just marinate it overnight in a mixture of oil and vinegar.

- 2 boneless strip steaks (about ¾ pound each)
- Cracked black pepper
- 1 baguette
- Olive oil
- 1 clove garlic
- Salt
- ¼ pound Roquefort
- Caramelized Shallots
- 1 sprig rosemary

1. Trim excess fat from steaks. Dry them well, coat all sides with cracked pepper, and refrigerate until needed.
2. Split the baguette in half lengthwise. Toast in the oven until golden brown. Drizzle with olive oil and rub lightly with the garlic clove.
3. Heat a cast-iron skillet over high heat and sear the steaks on both sides. Turn heat down to medium and cook to desired doneness, about 3 to 4 minutes per side for medium rare. Sprinkle with salt and let steaks sit for 5 minutes.
4. Cut toasted baguette into 4 equal pieces. Make 4 sandwiches, placing thinly sliced steak atop slices of Roquefort, then sprinkling with Caramelized Shallots and rosemary. Serve immediately.

CARAMELIZED SHALLOTS

makes about 1 cup

Leftover shallots will keep for several days in the refrigerator and can be used in omelets, pizzas, sautés, and sandwiches.

- 10 large or 15 small shallots
- 1 teaspoon olive oil
- 1 teaspoon unsalted butter
- 1 teaspoon sugar
- Salt and freshly ground pepper

1. Peel the shallots and cut lengthwise into ⅛-inch slices.
2. Heat oil in a small sauté pan over medium heat. Add the butter and shallots. Sprinkle with sugar and add salt and pepper to taste.
3. Cook the shallots until they begin to brown evenly, then turn the heat down to low and continue to cook until shallots are very soft, about 10 minutes. Serve at room temperature.

BANANAS in BROWN SUGAR and RUM

serves 4

Be very careful to stand away from the stove when you add the rum—the flames will be brief but dramatic.

- 4 bananas, ripe but firm
- 2 tablespoons unsalted butter
- 4 tablespoons dark brown sugar
- ½ cup dark rum (see Note)
- Crème fraîche or sour cream, for topping

1. Peel bananas and carefully cut in half lengthwise.
2. In a medium sauté pan over medium heat, melt 1 tablespoon of the butter. Add 2 tablespoons of the brown sugar and swirl until dissolved.
3. Add 2 of the bananas, cut side down, and cook for about 2 minutes on each side, turning very carefully.
4. Pouring from a measuring cup, with the pan off the heat, add ¼ cup of the rum. Stand back from the stove and return pan to the heat. Shake the pan, allowing the rum to ignite. Let the alcohol burn off and again shake the pan, to coat the bananas. Cook 1 minute longer, or until bananas are glazed and translucent.
5. Remove bananas to warm plates, divide sauce between them, and repeat with the other 2 bananas.
6. Garnish each banana with a little dab of crème fraîche or sour cream and serve immediately.

NOTE: *If you prefer not to use alcohol, substitute apple cider. Remove the bananas from the pan before adding the cider, and reduce until thick, about 3 minutes. Then return the bananas to the pan and proceed as directed in step 4.*

3

HERBED SPAETZLE
and SPINACH

ROASTED BEETS
with ORANGE and GINGER

SHELL STEAK with
SHIITAKE MUSHROOM SAUCE

APPLE BROWN BETTY

PREPARATION SCHEDULE

1 Roast beets and make
   vinaigrette.

2 Make spaetzle batter;
   wash spinach.

3 Assemble apple betty.

4 Cook spaetzle; toss beets
   with vinaigrette.

5 Cook steak and make sauce;
   sauté spinach and spaetzle.

6 Place apple betty in oven.

HERBED SPAETZLE and SPINACH

serves 4

These tiny dumplings are easy to make.

2½ cups all-purpose flour
    Salt and freshly ground pepper
½   teaspoon freshly grated nutmeg
1   teaspoon minced fresh rosemary
1   teaspoon minced fresh thyme leaves
1   tablespoon minced fresh parsley
⅔   cup milk
5   large eggs
6½ tablespoons olive oil
½   bunch spinach (about 1 pound),
    washed thoroughly and stems
    removed

1. Whisk together flour, 1 teaspoon salt, ⅛ teaspoon pepper, nutmeg, and herbs in a large bowl. In another bowl, beat the milk, eggs, and 5 tablespoons olive oil. Whisk into flour mixture until smooth.
2. In a large pot, bring 6 quarts of water to a boil; add 1 tablespoon salt. Fill a potato ricer fitted with a ¼-inch-hole attachment with batter and push it through into the boiling water, or use a colander, pushing batter through with a rubber spatula. Cook spaetzle until it floats to the top, about 30 seconds. Drain spaetzle in colander.
3. Heat remaining 1½ tablespoons olive oil in a skillet over medium-high heat. Add spinach and sauté until it starts to wilt. Add spaetzle, season with salt and pepper, and cook until hot. Serve immediately.

SHELL STEAK with SHIITAKE MUSHROOM SAUCE

serves 4

Shell steak is sometimes called New York strip steak.

2 1-pound boneless shell steaks
   Salt and freshly ground pepper
1 tablespoon chopped fresh savory,
   plus sprigs for garnish, or 1
   teaspoon dried
½ tablespoon unsalted butter
½ tablespoon olive oil
3 large cloves garlic
½ pound shiitake mushrooms,
   stems removed
½ cup dry red wine
1 cup beef stock, preferably
   homemade

1. Rub both sides of the steaks with salt, pepper, and savory. Heat the butter and oil in a large, heavy skillet over medium-high heat and add the garlic cloves and steaks. Lower heat to medium and cook the steaks 4 to 6 minutes on each side for medium rare. Transfer the steaks to a cutting board. Add the mushrooms to the pan, raise heat to high, and sauté for 2 minutes on each side. Transfer mushrooms to a small bowl.
2. Discard the garlic and fat from the pan. Add the red wine and stock to the pan. Reduce over high heat, scraping bottom with a wooden spoon, until ½ cup of sauce remains. Combine with the mushrooms.
3. Cut the beef crosswise into ¼-inch-thick slices and serve with the mushroom sauce on the side.

This ideal winter meal—shell steak, spaetzle, and roasted beets—is served on aqua-and-silver dinner plates with blond-wood-handled flatware.

Apple brown betty is baked in individual ramekins, then served on 1930s Wedgwood painted creamware.

ROASTED BEETS WITH ORANGE AND GINGER

serves 4

Roasting the beets concentrates their sweet flavor.

4   medium beets (about 1½ pounds), trimmed and scrubbed
3   tablespoons olive oil
    Salt and freshly ground pepper
1   medium orange
1½ teaspoons sherry vinegar
¾   teaspoon grated fresh ginger, or to taste
¼   cup pecan halves, toasted and broken in half lengthwise

1. Heat oven to 425°. Lay a large piece of aluminum foil on a baking sheet and place beets in the center. Drizzle with 1 tablespoon olive oil and season with salt and pepper. Wrap foil loosely around beets and roast in oven until beets are tender when pierced with a fork, about 1 hour. Let stand until cool enough to handle.
2. Using a zester, remove a quarter of the orange rind in long, thin strips. Cut away remaining rind and pith with a sharp knife. Remove segments from half the orange and cut them in half crosswise; set aside. Squeeze juice from remaining half and place 1 tablespoon of juice in a small bowl. Add vinegar and ginger and whisk in remaining 2 tablespoons olive oil. Season with salt and pepper.
3. Peel beets and quarter them; toss in a bowl with vinaigrette. Mix with orange segments, zest, and pecans, reserving some of each to sprinkle on top as a garnish.

APPLE BROWN BETTY

serves 4

Inverting this dessert shows off the layers of tart apples.

3   Granny Smith apples, peeled, cored and sliced ¼ inch thick
2   tablespoons fresh lemon juice
4½   tablespoons unsalted butter, melted
4   teaspoons granulated sugar
2   cups fresh bread crumbs
¼   cup firmly packed light-brown sugar
1   tablespoon all-purpose flour
⅛   teaspoon ground mace
½   teaspoon ground cinnamon
1   tablespoon cognac

1. Heat oven to 375°. In a large bowl, toss the apples with lemon juice. Brush 4 six-ounce ramekins with ½ tablespoon melted butter and sprinkle with the granulated sugar to coat.
2. In a small bowl, combine the bread crumbs with 4 tablespoons melted butter. Add remaining ingredients to the apples and toss. Divide a third of the bread crumbs among the ramekins. Arrange half the apples over bread crumbs and add another third of the crumbs. Repeat with the rest of the apples and bread crumbs. Press into ramekins.
3. Bake for 20 minutes. Raise oven temperature to 450°; continue baking until tops are golden brown and apples are tender, about 15 minutes. Remove from oven; cool for 5 minutes. Run a knife around sides of ramekins and turn apple betty out onto dessert plates.

MAKING THE GRADE

In the 1930s, the United States Department of Agriculture established a meat-grading system that set the standards of quality in this country. Although there are eight grades of beef, most of what is sold to the public is either prime, choice, or select, the top three grades. Prime beef is rich and well-marbled (marbling refers to the small flecks of fat throughout meat), and is most often found in restaurants and specialty butcher shops. Choice beef, though not as tender as prime, makes up 60 percent of what is sold in retail stores. Select cuts can also be found in supermarkets, but since they have less fat than either prime or choice, they're going to be somewhat tougher. Beef that is bought in the supermarket is stamped either "choice" or "select." Ground beef is not graded, but must adhere to USDA inspection codes.

There are certain qualities to look for in a piece of beef: The color of the meat should be a deep red and the fat a creamy white. Once beef is exposed to oxygen, it will turn from darker red to bright red, which does not affect its quality.

4

PREPARATION SCHEDULE

1 Prepare gratin and bake.

2 Infuse vanilla syrup and cut pears.

3 Brown sausage and keep warm.

4 Sauté pears, add syrup and figs, and bake.

5 Prepare red-onion mixture and heat with sausage.

6 Sauté broccoli rabe.

LEFT: Celeriac, an often-neglected root vegetable, makes a good base for this gratin, baked in a terracotta dish.

SAUSAGE WITH STEWED RED ONIONS

1. In a cast-iron skillet over medium heat, brown the sausage in oil on all sides, about 20 minutes. Remove from pan and keep warm. Do not wash pan.

2. Cook the onions in same pan over medium heat, stirring often, until tender and translucent, about 15 minutes.

3. Add the vinegar and cook 1 minute. Add water, salt, pepper, and whole rosemary leaves, and cook over medium-high heat, scraping bottom of pan, until liquid is reduced by half.

4. Lower heat to a simmer and return the sausage to the pan. Simmer together with the onions for 5 to 10 minutes. Serve immediately.

1. Heat oven to 400°. Butter a 1½-quart gratin dish. Scatter shallots over bottom of dish. Trim celeriac by cutting off bottom and top, then cutting off thick outer layer with a sharp knife. Cut into ¼-inch slices and then julienne. Arrange evenly in gratin dish. Sprinkle thyme leaves over celeriac.

2. In a small bowl, whisk together the cream, mustard, nutmeg, and salt and pepper. Pour over the celeriac and sprinkle with cheeses. Cover with foil and bake for 20 minutes.

3. Remove foil and continue baking until top is brown and bubbly and cream is thickened and reduced, about 20 more minutes. Let cool for 10 minutes and serve.

SAUSAGE WITH STEWED RED ONIONS

serves 4 to 6

Most butchers make a variety of sausages, including veal, chicken, and turkey, in addition to the more traditional pork. Use your favorite for this recipe.

2 pounds sausage (we used veal)
1 teaspoon olive oil
2 large red onions, cut into ¼-inch slices
1 tablespoon red-wine vinegar
1 cup water
  Salt and freshly ground pepper
1 sprig fresh rosemary

CELERIAC GRATIN

serves 4 to 6

Celeriac is also known as celery root. Look for medium-size bulbs that are firm and heavy.

4 shallots, sliced thin
3 medium bulbs celeriac
2 sprigs fresh thyme
1 cup heavy cream
1 tablespoon Dijon mustard
  Freshly grated nutmeg
  Salt and freshly ground pepper
¾ cup freshly grated Gruyère
¼ cup freshly grated Parmesan

SAUTÉED BROCCOLI RABE

serves 4 to 6

This leafy relative of broccoli has a pleasant sharpness, but it can become too bitter if it's overcooked.

2 bunches broccoli rabe
2 cloves garlic, sliced thin
1 tablespoon olive oil
  Salt and freshly ground pepper
  Lemon wedges (optional)

1. Trim large stems from the broccoli rabe and discard. Wash and leave slightly wet. In a large saucepan with a lid, cook the garlic in oil over medium-low heat until golden brown.

2. Add the broccoli rabe to the pot, turn heat to medium high, sprinkle with salt, and cover. Remove lid to stir every minute or so until rabe is completely wilted, about 5 minutes. Season with pepper and fresh lemon juice if desired.

BAKED VANILLA PEARS
with FIGS
serves 4 to 6

Look for dried figs that are soft and moist.

1 vanilla bean
¼ cup plus 2 tablespoons sugar
¾ cup water
3 firm Bartlett pears
2 tablespoons butter
2 dried black mission figs

1. Heat oven to 400°. Split vanilla bean lengthwise and set one half aside. Scrape seeds from other half into a small saucepan, and add the pod, ¼ cup sugar, and the water. Bring to a boil, then simmer 10 minutes to infuse vanilla flavor into syrup. Strain and set aside.

2. Peel the pears and cut in half lengthwise, leaving stems on. Cut out core, scooping out a little extra flesh. Trim off a little flesh on round side so that halves will lie nicely on a plate.

3. In a large sauté pan over medium heat, melt butter. Add remaining 2 tablespoons sugar and stir until melted.

4. Add pears, cut side down, and cook until brown, shaking pan occasionally. Turn over and cook a few minutes more. Transfer to a baking dish, and pour vanilla syrup over pears. Add other half of vanilla bean. Slice figs lengthwise and put 1 or 2 slices in center of each pear. Spoon a little syrup over figs and bake until soft and tender, about 30 minutes, depending on ripeness of pears. Serve hot or warm.

ABOVE RIGHT: Stewed red onions add a slightly sweet flavor to a cast-iron skillet of veal sausage.

RIGHT: A squirt of lemon juice is the finishing touch to sautéed broccoli rabe, served on a French creamware platter.

OPPOSITE: Rustic French pottery, placed on top of a fringed linen-cotton throw, perfectly suits this earthy meal. A George IV silver fork is paired with a Tiffany Flemish dinner knife; the mustard pot is yellow ware.
THIS PAGE: A black mission fig tops a baked pear in a deep, white porcelain plate from Japan.

5

ENDIVE and
GRAINY MUSTARD SALAD

POTATO and GREENS SOUP

RED CABBAGE and
ONION TARTS

PINEAPPLE in BROWN SUGAR
with ICE CREAM

PREPARATION SCHEDULE

1 Assemble all ingredients
 and utensils.

2 Make pastry; chill.

3 Prepare tart filling; while it
 cooks, prepare pineapple.

4 Prepare leeks; cook.

5 Add stock and potatoes;
 simmer.

6 While soup cooks, assemble
 tarts. Chill, then bake.

7 While tarts bake, puree soup;
 simmer.

7 Assemble salad.

8 Add greens to soup.

9 Cook pineapple; serve with
 ice cream.

LEFT: Try making this soup using a combination of bitter greens, such as arugula and escarole. A copper saucepan adds a homey touch.

3. Ladle about 3 cups of soup into a blender (don't fill more than halfway). Hold the lid on with a dish towel to prevent splattering, and blend until smooth. Return pureed soup to saucepan, stir to combine, and bring back to a simmer. Season to taste.

4. Stir in the greens. Cook for 2 to 3 minutes, until wilted and bright green, and serve immediately.

POTATO and GREENS SOUP

serves 4

If you want to make the soup ahead of time, prepare through step 3. Reheat and stir in the greens just before serving.

 1 tablespoon olive oil
 1 tablespoon unsalted butter
 1 bunch leeks, thoroughly rinsed
 and thinly sliced (about 2 cups)
 4½ cups chicken stock, preferably
 homemade
 Salt and freshly ground pepper
 8 white potatoes (about 3½ pounds),
 peeled and cut into ¾-inch cubes
 1 bunch arugula or other bitter
 greens such as curly endive or
 escarole, washed

1. Heat the oil and butter in a large, heavy saucepan over low heat. Add the leeks and stir well. Cover and cook until soft, about 5 minutes.

2. Add stock and bring to a simmer over medium-high heat. Add salt and pepper to taste. Add potatoes and bring back to a simmer. Cook until tender but not mushy, 10 to 15 minutes. Turn off heat.

ENDIVE and GRAINY MUSTARD SALAD

serves 4

Belgian endive should be pale yellow with white edges. If the leaves are turning green or have brown spots, they aren't fresh.

 6 heads Belgian endive
 2 hard-boiled eggs
 1 tablespoon chopped flat-leaf parsley
 1 teaspoon grainy mustard
 1 teaspoon red-wine vinegar
 4 teaspoons extra-virgin olive oil
 Salt and freshly ground pepper

1. Remove the large outer leaves from endives and set aside. Slice remaining endive crosswise and set aside. Chop eggs and mix with parsley. Set aside.

2. Combine mustard and vinegar. Slowly whisk in olive oil, and season with salt and pepper. Mix dressing with sliced endive.

3. Arrange whole endive leaves on four plates and place a mound of dressed endive in center of each. Garnish with egg-parsley mixture and serve.

Grainy mustard has a stronger flavor than smooth mustard and is well suited to the endive's slight bite.

Antique finger bowls do double duty for serving the warm pineapple and vanilla ice cream.

PINEAPPLE in BROWN SUGAR
with ICE CREAM

serves 4

Choose a sweet-smelling pineapple that yields to gentle pressure but doesn't have soft spots.

1 tablespoon unsalted butter
2-3 tablespoons dark brown sugar
1 pineapple, peeled, cored, and cut into 1¼-inch cubes
2 tablespoons rum (optional)
½ vanilla bean, split and scraped, or 1 teaspoon vanilla extract
1 pint vanilla ice cream

1. Melt butter in a medium sauté pan over low heat. Add sugar and stir until melted. Add pineapple, rum, if desired, and vanilla, and turn heat up to medium high.
2. Cook, stirring, until liquid is reduced and pineapple is glazed, about 15 minutes. Be careful not to burn.
3. Serve the pineapple in bowls with a scoop of ice cream.

BELOW: A paisley shawl makes a richly colored tablecloth. Dinner is served on a mix of modern and vintage gold-rimmed dishes; the silver is German.

RED CABBAGE and ONION TARTS

serves 4

The pastry for these little tarts can be molded free-form instead of in flan rings.

2½ cups all-purpose flour
Salt and freshly ground pepper
3 tablespoons fresh thyme leaves
½ pound (2 sticks) unsalted butter, cut up
¼-½ cup ice water, plus ½ cup water for filling
2 tablespoons olive oil
2 red onions, sliced ¼ inch thick
¼ head red cabbage, shredded
2 tablespoons red-wine vinegar
1 teaspoon sugar
¼ pound Gruyère or Swiss cheese, cubed

1. Combine flour, 1 teaspoon salt, ½ teaspoon pepper, and 1 tablespoon thyme in a food processor. Add butter and process until mixture resembles coarse meal, about 10 seconds. Slowly pour in ice water with motor running until mixture holds together when squeezed. Wrap in plastic and press into a flat disk. Chill until firm.
2. Heat oil in a large sauté pan over medium heat. Add onions; cook until soft. Add cabbage; reduce heat. Add ½ cup water, 2 tablespoons thyme, vinegar, sugar, salt, and pepper. Cover; cook 10 minutes. Uncover, turn heat up, and cook until liquid is gone.
3. Heat oven to 425°. Quarter dough and roll into 5-inch circles. Fit into 4-inch flan rings. Add filling and scatter cheese on top. Fold over pastry edges. Chill until firm. Bake 15 to 20 minutes; serve hot.

6

WINTER CRUDITÉ SALAD

ROASTED FENNEL and
POTATOES

HALIBUT with
PUTTANESCA SAUCE

CHOCOLATE TURNOVERS

PREPARATION SCHEDULE

1 Cut vegetables and make vinaigrette.

2 Prepare ingredients for puttanesca sauce.

3 Roll out puff pastry; prepare and freeze turnovers.

4 Roast fennel and potatoes.

5 Cook halibut and make sauce.

6 Toss salad with vinaigrette.

7 After dinner, brush turnovers with egg wash and bake.

WINTER CRUDITÉ SALAD

serves 4

*Choose a celery root that seems
heavy for its size.*

½ teaspoon Dijon mustard

1½ teaspoons sherry vinegar

1½ tablespoons extra-virgin olive oil
Salt and freshly ground pepper

1 celery root (about ¾ pound)

4 carrots, cut into 2½-inch
julienne strips

8 red radishes (about ½ pound),
thinly sliced

1. In a small bowl, combine mustard and vinegar. Whisk in olive oil until the mixture is creamy. Season with salt and pepper.

2. Peel celery root with a sharp knife. Cut root in half crosswise and slice each half as thinly as possible. Keep slices in a bowl of cold water until needed. Drain and pat dry when ready to toss with the vinaigrette.

3. Place the vegetables in separate bowls, season with salt and pepper, and toss well. Add about 1½ teaspoons dressing to each bowl and toss again. Arrange the vegetables in separate piles on salad plates and serve immediately.

HALIBUT with
PUTTANESCA SAUCE

serves 4

*Halibut is the perfect foil
for this robust sauce.*

1 28-ounce can plum tomatoes

3 tablespoons olive oil

2 cloves garlic, minced (about 1
teaspoon)

1 large onion, thinly sliced

⅓ cup oil-cured black olives,
halved and pitted

2 tablespoons capers

4 anchovy fillets, rinsed and minced

1 teaspoon finely chopped fresh
rosemary

4 halibut steaks (about 6 to 8
ounces each)
Salt and freshly ground pepper

⅓ cup chopped flat-leaf parsley

1. Drain tomatoes, reserving ½ cup liquid. Seed and coarsely chop tomatoes. Heat 1½ tablespoons olive oil in a large skillet over medium-low heat. Add garlic and cook until aromatic, 1 to 2 minutes. Add onion and cook until transparent, about 5 minutes. Raise heat to medium high, add tomatoes, reserved liquid, olives, capers, anchovies, and rosemary and cook, stirring often, 2 to 3 minutes. Remove from heat and set aside.

2. Heat remaining oil in a large nonstick skillet over medium-high heat. Season both sides of halibut steaks with salt and pepper. Cook steaks until golden brown, 4 to 5 minutes on each side.

3. Reheat the sauce until it simmers. Stir in parsley. Serve the halibut with a little sauce on each steak.

ABOVE LEFT: The winter crudité salad looks especially pretty on a Paris-porcelain cake plate.

LEFT: Halibut, available year-round, has firm white flesh and a mild flavor.

A square of chocolate enclosed in flaky puff pastry is an after-dinner version of the classic pain au chocolat. The turnovers are served on a French salad plate with a gold-leaf rim.

LEFT: Raw fennel looks like a bulbous celery heart; when cooked, its anise flavor goes well with the milder potatoes.

ROASTED FENNEL and POTATOES

serves 4

Preheat the roasting pan to give the vegetables a crisp, golden crust.

2 fennel bulbs (about 4 ounces each), trimmed
8 red potatoes (about 1 pound), cut in half
  Salt and freshly ground pepper
1 tablespoon olive oil

1. Heat oven to 425°. Set a heavy roasting pan in the oven and allow to preheat for 20 minutes.
2. Meanwhile, cut each fennel bulb lengthwise into six wedges. Season fennel and potatoes with salt and pepper and toss with olive oil.
3. Remove the roasting pan from the oven and place fennel and potatoes, cut side down, in the hot pan. Return pan to oven and roast the vegetables for 30 minutes, without turning, until tender and golden brown. Serve immediately.

CHOCOLATE TURNOVERS

makes 9

Frozen puff pastry can be found in the freezer section of most supermarkets.

1 9½-inch-square sheet of puff pastry, thawed according to package directions
1 egg yolk
2 tablespoons heavy cream
2¼ ounces semisweet chocolate, cut into 9 pieces

1. Heat oven to 400°. Place puff pastry on a lightly floured work surface. Sprinkle the pastry with a little more flour and roll out to form a 12-inch square. Brush away any excess flour and trim the edges to make a perfect square.
2. Cut puff pastry into nine 3½-inch squares and transfer them to a parchment-lined baking sheet. Discard excess.
3. In a small bowl, whisk together egg yolk and heavy cream. Neatly brush a little of the egg wash along 2 adjacent edges of each square. Place a piece of chocolate just below the center of each square and fold down unwashed edges to enclose chocolate and form a triangle. Using your fingers, gently but firmly press puff-pastry edges together to seal.
4. Place baking sheet in freezer for 20 minutes, or until pastry is chilled. Remove from freezer and brush tops liberally with remaining egg wash. Place in oven and bake until triangles are puffed and golden brown, about 15 minutes.

SWEET TALK

The Aztec emperor Montezuma drank fifty goblets of hot chocolate every day. His version had the consistency of honey and was flavored with chile peppers. In 1519, when Hernando Cortés conquered Mexico, he brought back some cacao (now called cocoa) beans to Spain, where they were mixed with sugar and spices to make a palatable drink. It wasn't until the nineteenth century, though, that people discovered that chocolate could be eaten solid.

Today, most of the world's cocoa crop comes from Africa and Brazil. The cocoa beans are dried, roasted, and ground, then converted into a thick paste called chocolate liquor, which is composed of cocoa solids and a light yellow fat called cocoa butter. Cocoa butter gives chocolate its richness, so the finest-quality chocolate always contains a high proportion. Unsweetened chocolate is used primarily in baking. Bitter-, or semisweet, chocolate (also called dark chocolate) contains enough sugar to be eaten alone. Milk chocolate (eating chocolate) is rarely used for cooking. White chocolate contains cocoa butter but no chocolate solids, and is similar in texture to regular chocolate.

7

CELERIAC SLAW

OVEN FRIES

TENDERLOINS
with MUSTARD SAUCE

BAKED APPLE WEDGES

PREPARATION SCHEDULE

1 Cut and bake fries.

2 Blanch celeriac and make dressing.

3 Coat tenderloins with pepper.

4 Coat apples with oatmeal-nut crust.

5 Cook steaks; dress celeriac; make mustard sauce.

6 Place apples in oven.

OVEN FRIES

serves 4

These fries are baked and not deep-fried, so the fat content is much lower than in regular fries.

4 potatoes, preferably Yukon Gold or russet

2 tablespoons olive oil

6 sprigs fresh thyme, or 2 teaspoons dried
   Salt and freshly ground pepper

1. Heat oven to 425°. Cut potatoes lengthwise into thick slices, then into ½-inch-by-½-inch-thick strips. Place in a bowl of cold water until ready to use. Drain and dry well on paper towels.

2. Toss potatoes with oil and spread out on a dark roasting pan or baking sheet. Scatter thyme over potatoes. Bake for 35 to 40 minutes, turning occasionally, until potatoes are brown and crisp on all sides.

3. Remove the potatoes from oven and discard thyme stems (the leaves will have fallen off). Sprinkle potatoes with salt and pepper and serve immediately.

TENDERLOINS
with MUSTARD SAUCE

serves 4

Serve the steaks with a fresh green salad—we used an assortment of red and green lettuces—dressed with a simple vinaigrette.

4 tenderloin steaks, 4 ounces each

3 tablespoons coarsely ground pepper, or to taste

2 shallots, peeled

¼ cup brandy

1 tablespoon Dijon mustard

⅓ cup heavy cream
   Salt

1. Heat oven to 350°. Coat steaks with pepper on both sides. Heat a cast-iron skillet over medium heat until very hot. Sear steaks for 5 minutes on each side, then transfer to oven to finish cooking, about 8 minutes for medium rare. Transfer to a plate to rest while you make the sauce.

2. Mince shallots and cook over low heat in the same skillet that steaks were cooked in. Add brandy and cook, stirring constantly, for 1 minute, or until reduced to 1 tablespoon. Stir in mustard and cream. Bring to a simmer and season to taste with salt and pepper. Serve sauce alongside the steaks.

BELOW: The mustard sauce is served in a Venetian-glass bowl.

This menu of tenderloin and oven fries was inspired by the French bistro combination of "steak frites." The dinner, side, and candle plates are nineteenth-century Wedding Band; the goblet is Venetian glass.

ABOVE: Long ribbons of celeriac are a departure from the shredded cabbage of summer coleslaws. The slaw is served in a Wedgwood drabware dish.

salted water. Squeeze out water; set aside.

2. Peel celery and slice on an angle as thinly as possible. Set aside.

3. In a blender or food processor, combine buttermilk, oil, lemon juice, and salt and pepper to taste. Process until smooth. Add capers and herbs and process 5 to 10 seconds, until coarsely chopped.

4. Combine celeriac and celery in a bowl and toss with the dressing.

CELERIAC SLAW

serves 4

A light, low-fat buttermilk dressing replaces the rich remoulade sauce in this version of the bistro classic céleri rémoulade.

2 medium bulbs celeriac (celery root), 1½-2 pounds total

2 stalks celery

½ cup low-fat buttermilk

2 tablespoons vegetable oil

1 tablespoon fresh lemon juice
Salt and freshly ground pepper

2 tablespoons capers, rinsed

1 tablespoon chopped fresh chervil, or 1 teaspoon dried

1 tablespoon chopped fresh tarragon, or 1 teaspoon dried

1. Peel celeriac with a paring knife. Cut into 1-inch-thick slices, then cut into very thin ribbons (use a mandoline if you have one), placing in cold water to prevent browning. Drain. Blanch briefly in boiling

BAKED APPLE WEDGES

serves 4

McIntosh apples have the best texture for this easy dessert because they become soft without falling apart.

3 tablespoons dark brown sugar

½ cup rolled oats (not instant)

¼ teaspoon cinnamon

¼ teaspoon ground ginger
Pinch of ground nutmeg
Pinch of ground cloves

¼ cup sliced almonds, toasted

4 McIntosh apples

1 large egg beaten with 1 tablespoon milk
Whipped cream or ice cream, optional
Fresh mint leaves, as garnish

1. Heat oven to 350°. Sprinkle 1 tablespoon brown sugar over a baking sheet. Combine oats, remaining 2 tablespoons sugar, and spices in the work bowl of a food processor and blend until smooth. Add half the almonds and process until finely chopped. Add remaining almonds; process until coarsely chopped. Transfer to a shallow bowl.

2. Peel apples and cut into quarters. Cut out cores. Dip apples into egg mixture, letting excess drip off. Coat well with the oatmeal-nut mixture and transfer to prepared baking sheet.

3. Bake for 20 to 25 minutes, or until soft. Serve warm with whipped cream or ice cream, if desired. Garnish with mint leaves.

McIntosh apples, coated with an oat-meal nut crust, are baked until golden brown and then served with whipped cream on a Venetian-style green-and-gold glass plate.

ROASTED BARLEY PILAF

CITRUS MARINATED
PORK CHOPS

SAUTÉED GREEN APPLES
and LEEKS

WINTER FRUIT SALAD

PREPARATION SCHEDULE

1 Assemble all ingredients and utensils.

2 Marinate pork chops.

3 Pan-roast barley for pilaf; add shallots, mushrooms, and stock.

4 While pilaf simmers, remove pork chops from marinade and cook.

5 Sauté green apples and leeks.

6 Assemble salad.

ROASTED BARLEY PILAF

serves 4

*Pan-roasting the barley gives it
a rich, nutty flavor.*

1   tablespoon olive oil
1   cup pearl barley, rinsed
2   shallots, peeled and minced
¼   pound white or wild mushrooms,
     sliced
2   cups low-sodium chicken stock
     or water
¾   teaspoon salt
     Freshly ground pepper

1. In a heavy, medium saucepan, heat oil over medium heat. Add the barley and cook, stirring frequently, for 10 minutes. The barley should start to brown and give off an aroma.
2. Add shallots and cook for 2 minutes. Add mushrooms and cook until wilted, 2 to 3 minutes. Add stock or water and salt. Bring to a boil; then turn down heat to a bare simmer. Cover and cook for 45 minutes, or until liquid is absorbed.
3. Stir well, season with pepper and more salt, if needed, and serve immediately.

CITRUS MARINATED
PORK CHOPS

serves 4

*You can put the chops in the
marinade in the morning and refrigerate
until ready to cook.*

     Juice of 2 limes
     Juice of 2 oranges
1½ tablespoons balsamic vinegar
1   tablespoon Dijon mustard
2-3 cloves garlic, peeled and crushed
2-3 sprigs fresh thyme or ½ teaspoon
     dried thyme
½   teaspoon salt
½   teaspoon cracked black pepper
1   tablespoon plus 1 teaspoon olive oil
4   center-cut pork chops, 1 inch thick
1   tablespoon unsalted butter

1. In a large, nonreactive bowl, combine all ingredients except the 1 teaspoon olive oil, pork chops, and butter; mix well. Add chops, and spoon marinade over them to coat. Marinate for at least 30 minutes.
2. Heat a heavy skillet over medium heat for 2 minutes. Remove chops from marinade, reserving marinade. Brush pan with the teaspoon of oil; cook chops for 5 minutes on each side. Add marinade, lower heat, and cook, covered, for 7 minutes, turning chops once.
3. Remove chops from pan and set aside. Turn up heat to medium high; reduce liquid until thick. Remove from heat, stir in butter, and strain. Pour sauce over chops; serve immediately.

SAUTÉED GREEN APPLES
and LEEKS

serves 4

*To clean leeks thoroughly, soak them in cold
water for five to ten minutes, then lift them out
of the water, leaving the dirt behind.*

2   large leeks, white part only
2   teaspoons unsalted butter
2   large green apples such as
     Granny Smith, quartered, cored,
     and thinly sliced

1. Split the leeks in half lengthwise, leaving a little of the root end intact so they stay together. Wash well and dry. Cut leeks into thin strips about 2 inches long.
2. In a medium sauté pan over medium heat, melt 1 teaspoon butter. Add the leeks and cook until soft, about 3 minutes. Remove leeks from pan and set aside.
3. Melt the remaining teaspoon butter and add apple slices. Turn heat to high and cook until apples are lightly browned and soft, about 3 minutes. Return leeks to pan and toss together. Serve immediately.

WINTER FRUIT SALAD

serves 4

*Papayas and strawberries are
widely available in the late winter months and
make a refreshing and light dessert.*

1   pink papaya
1   yellow papaya
1   pint fresh strawberries
1   lime, halved
     Fresh mint, as garnish

1. Peel papayas; scoop out seeds and discard. Wash strawberries and remove hulls.
2. Slice the strawberries in half, or in quarters if very large. Cut one of the papayas into 1-inch chunks and the other into long strips ½ inch wide.
3. Squeeze lime halves over fruit, garnish with fresh mint leaves, and serve.

OPPOSITE: Blue plates by Schammell, which hold the pork chops, apples and leeks, and pilaf, are placed on Wedgwood Queensplain dinner plates. The polka-dot glasses are by Fenton; the blue goblets are from the 1940s. THIS PAGE: Winter-fruit salad is served in a pressed-glass compote.

the guide

spring

page 15

Victorian silver **dessert spoon** by William Pope, $50, George III silver **dessert fork**, $75, *both at I. Freeman & Son, 60 East 56th Street, New York, NY 10022; 212-759-6900.* 10½"-by-14" porcelain **tart pan** by Apilco, $85, *at Lamalle Kitchenware, 36 West 25th Street, New York, NY 10010; 212-242-0750 or 800-660-0750. Catalogue, $3.*

pages 16, 18

Antique **soy-sauce dish**, $45, and celadon **teacups**, $50 each, *both at Gordon Foster, 1322 Third Avenue, New York, NY 10021; 212-744-4922.* Large beige **low bowls** by Stewart, $90 each, *at Gordon Foster, 1322 Third Avenue, New York, NY 10021; 212-744-4922.* **Chopsticks**, $10 per pair, *at Felissimo, 10 West 56th Street, New York, NY 10019; 212-956-4438 or 800-565-6785.*

page 18

Bronze **vase**, $125, and small beige **low**
bowl by Stewart, $55, *both at Gordon Foster, 1322 Third Avenue, New York, NY 10021; 212-744-4922.*

page 19

Marble plate, $150, *at Gordon Foster, 1322 Third Avenue, New York, NY 10021; 212-744-4922.*

page 20

Porcelain **bowl**, $75, *at Takashimaya, 693 Fifth Avenue, New York, NY 10022; 800-753-2038.*

page 21

Wineglass, $46, *at Simon Pearce, 500 Park Avenue at 59th Street, New York, NY 10022; 212-421-8801.* French **flatware**, $185 for 5-piece setting, *at Takashimaya, 693 Fifth Avenue, New York, NY 10022; 800-753-2038.*

page 24

8" **steamer**, $2.99, *at Bridge Kitchenware, 214 East 52nd Street, New York, NY 10022; 212-838-1901. Catalogue, $3.*

page 25

Soup bowls, from a selection, $12.50 to $18, *at Dean & DeLuca, 560 Broadway, New York, NY 10012; 800-221-7714 or 212-431-1691.*

pages 25, 26

Antique **spoon**, $165 for set of 6, *at Wolfman-Gold & Good Co., 116 Greene Street, New York, NY 10012; 212-431-1888.*

pages 25, 26, 27

Ecru **tablecloth** by Hemstidi, $140, *at ABC Carpet & Home, 888 Broadway, New York, NY 10003; 212-473-3000 or 800-888-7847 (outside NY, NJ, CT).*

page 26

Hotel-silver **fork**, $9, *at Henro, 525 Broome Street, New York, NY 10013; 212-343-0221.* **Whiskey glass** by Skrufs, $23, *at Lars Bolander Ltd., 5 Toilsome Lane, East Hampton, NY 11937; 516-329-3400.*

page 36

Hotel-silver **soup spoon**, $9, *at Henro, 525 Broome Street, New York, NY 10013; 212-343-0221.*

page 37

Poblano peppers, $26 for 10 pounds (minimum order), *available from Frieda's by Mail, P.O. Box 58488, Los Angeles, CA 90058; 800-241-1771.*

page 38

Celadon **dinner plates**, $75 each, and **bowl**, $65, *both at Gordon Foster, 1322 Third Avenue, New York, NY 10021; 212-744-4922.* **Napkin**, $27, *at Interieurs, 114 Wooster Street, New York, NY 10012; 212-343-0800.*

summer

page 43

Wheat **dinner plates**, $15 each, Homer Laughlin stoneware **pasta bowls**, $5.75 each, and **dinner plates**, $11.50, *all at Wolfman-Gold & Good Co., 116 Greene*

Street, New York, NY 10012; 212-431-1888.

page 46

1920s Sinclair **plate**, $55, linen **napkin**, $16 (set of 4), linen **table runners**, $25 to $35, *all from Fritz's American Wonder at the Tomato Factory, 2 Somerset Street, Hopewell, NJ 08525; 609-466-9833.*

page 47

Nineteenth-century English cut-panel **crystal wineglass**, $800 (set of 8), *at James II Galleries Ltd., 11 East 57th Street, 4th floor, New York, NY 10022; 212-355-7040.* Irish linen **table runner** (circa 1910), $26, Depression-glass **cake plate**, $35, Continental **silver fork**, $45, *all from Fritz's American Wonder at the Tomato Factory, 2 Somerset Street, Hopewell, NJ 08525; 609-466-9833.*

page 48

Irish linen **dish towel**, $8.50, *from Fritz's American Wonder at the Tomato Factory, 2 Somerset Street, Hopewell, NJ 08525; 609-466-9833.*

page 49

Continental hand-blown **plate**, $55, American damask **tabletop square**, $35, *both from Fritz's American Wonder at the Tomato Factory, 2 Somerset Street, Hopewell, NJ 08525; 609-466-9833.* 5" porcelain **tartlet dishes** by Apilco, $10 each, *available at Lamalle Kitchenware, 36 West 25th Street, New York, NY 10010; 212-242-0750 or 800-660-0750. Catalogue, $3.*

page 50

French-bistro steel **folding chairs** (set of 4), *at Pierre Deux Antiques, 369 Bleecker Street, New York, NY 10014; 212-243-7740. Prices upon request.*

page 54

1940s wrought-iron **café chairs**, $250 each, *at Paula Rubenstein Ltd., 65 Prince Street, New York, NY 10012; 212-966-8954.* **Dinner plates** by Wedgwood, $34 each. *Call 800-677-7860 for retailers. Free catalogue.* 1920s iridescent **tumblers**,

$10 each, *at Fran Jay's Depression Glass, 10 Church Street, Lambertville, NJ 08530; 609-397-1571.* Silver-plate **serving spoon** by Simeson H&M Co., $14, *from the Country Cupboard at the Tomato Factory, Railroad Place, Hopewell, NJ 08525; 609-466-9833.*

page 55

Silver-plate **citrus spoon** by Gorham, $12, *from the Country Cupboard at the Tomato Factory, Railroad Place, Hopewell, NJ 08525; 609-466-9833.*

page 60

Large tan linen **napkin** (used as tablecloth), $22, *at Ad Hoc Softwares, 410 West Broadway, New York, NY 10012; 212-925-2652.*

pages 62, 65

Hartland **wineglasses**, $46, *at Simon Pearce, 500 Park Avenue at 59th Street, New York, NY 10022; 212-421-8801.*

page 63

Vintage oversize **bowls** by Hall, $65 each, *at Fishs Eddy, 889 Broadway, New York, NY 10003; 212-420-9020.* Sterling-silver **cocktail forks**, $50, *at I. Freeman & Son, 60 East 56th Street, New York, NY 10022; 212-759-6900.* Vintage **pewter beaker** (with sunflowers), $125, *at Millbrook Antiques Mall, Franklin Avenue, P.O. Box 1271, Millbrook, NY 12545; 914-677-9311.*

page 66

French Baguette **silverware** by Chambly, $126 for 5-piece setting, *from Chelsea Passage at Barneys New York, 106 Seventh Avenue, New York, NY 10011; 212-339-7300.*

pages 66, 67

Linen **napkins**, *from a selection at Bergdorf Goodman, 754 Fifth Avenue, New York, NY 10019; 212-753-7300.*

page 67

Small **bowl**, $35, *at Simon Pearce, 500 Park Avenue at 59th Street, New York, NY 10022; 212-421-8801.*

page 68

9" **bowl** by Russel Wright, $85, *at Mood Indigo, 181 Prince Street, New York, NY 10012; 212-254-1176.*

page 69

8" **lunch plate** from the Highlight collection by Russel Wright, $42, *at Mood Indigo, 181 Prince Street, New York, NY 10012, 212-254-1176.*

pages 69, 70

4-prong English silver Irish Rib **dinner fork**, $245, handmade English silver Plain Spire **dinner knife**, $135, *both at James Robinson, 480 Park Avenue, New York, NY 10022; 212-752-6166.*

page 70

Highlight 10" **dinner plate** by Russel Wright, $55, *at Mood Indigo, 181 Prince Street, New York, NY 10012; 212-254-1176.* Perfection **white-wine glass**, $70, *from Baccarat. Call 800-845-1928 for nearest store locations.*

page 71

Celadon ceramic **bowl** by Palais Royal of France, $58, *at Takashimaya, 693 Fifth Avenue, New York, NY 10022; 800-753-2038.* Nineteenth-century Scandinavian **glass bowl**, $125, *at Evergreen Antiques, 1249 Third Avenue, New York, NY 10021; 212-744-5664.*

autumn

page 74

George III **salad fork**, $150, *at I. Freeman & Son, 60 East 56th Street, New York, NY 10022; 212-759-6900.* White **salad plate** by Wedgwood, $16.80. *Call 800-677-7860 for retailers.*

pages 74 to 77

French textured **tablecloth**, $125,

at Trouvaille Française, 212-737-6015 (by appointment only).

page 76

Elsa Peretti **crystal glass**, $22, *at Tiffany & Co., 727 Fifth Avenue, New York, NY 10022; 212-755-8000 or (outside New York) 800-526-0649.* White **soup bowl**, $40, and **dinner plate**, $24, both by Wedgwood. *Call 800-677-7860 for retailers.* George III **fork**, $150, *at I. Freeman & Son, 60 East 56th Street, New York, NY 10022; 212-759-6905.*

pages 76, 77

Linen **napkin**, $22, *at Bergdorf Goodman, 754 Fifth Avenue, New York, NY 10019; 212-759-6905.*

page 77

White **bread-and-butter plate** by Wedgwood, $11. *Call 800-677-7860 for retailers.* George III silver **teaspoons**, $70 each, *at I. Freeman & Son, 60 East 56th Street, New York, NY 10022; 212-759-6905.* China **custard cup** by Hall, $4.60, *at Bridge Kitchenware, 214 East 52nd Street, New York, NY 10022; 212-838-1901. Catalogue, $3.*

page 83

Nineteenth-century French **folding chair**, $675 each, *at Rooms & Gardens, 290 Lafayette Street, New York, NY 10012; 212-431-1297.* Coin-silver **tablespoon**, $65, *from the Country Cupboard at the Tomato Factory, Railroad Place, Hopewell, NJ 08525; 609-466-9833.* Linen **napkins**, $24 each, *from Lisa Hammerquist, 240 Sheridan Avenue, #2W, Albany, NY 12210; 518-434-9151.*

page 84

Farmington **butter knife**, $12, *from the Country Cupboard at the Tomato Factory, Railroad Place, Hopewell, NJ 08525; 609-466-9833.*

page 85

Ironstone **honey dish** by Wood & Son, $16, *from Linda Rosen Antiques at the Tomato Factory, Railroad Place,*

Hopewell, NJ 08525; 609-466-9833.

page 86

English ironstone **luncheon plate**, $50, *at David & Co., 192 Sixth Avenue, New York, NY 10013; 212-226-5717.*

page 87

Crystal glass by Elsa Peretti, $22, *at Tiffany & Co., 727 Fifth Avenue, New York, NY 10022; 212-755-8000 or 800-526-0649 (outside New York).* Clinton **dinner fork** by Tiffany, *at I. Freeman & Son, 60 East 56th Street, New York, NY 10022; 212-759-6900.* Restaurant-ware **dinner plate**, *at Wolfman-Gold & Good Co., 116 Greene Street, New York, NY 10012; 212-431-1888.* Linen **napkin**, $30, *at Felissimo, 10 West 56th Street, New York, NY 10019; 212-956-4438 or 800-565-6785.*

page 92

Nineteenth-century French **folding table**, $800, *at Rooms & Gardens, 290 Lafayette Street, New York, NY 10012; 212-431-1297.*

page 94

Antique linen damask **tablecloth**, $75, *at Trouvaille Française; 212-737-6015 (by appointment only).*

page 95

Embroidered linen **napkin** by Muriel Grateau, $28, *at Interieurs, 114 Wooster Street, New York, NY 10012; 212-343-0800.*

page 97

Linen **napkin** by Liz Wain, $30, *at Bergdorf Goodman, 754 Fifth Avenue, New York, NY 10019; 212-753-7300.*

page 98

Soup bowl by Joan Platt, $36, *at Claiborne, 452 West Broadway, New York, NY 10012; 212-475-3072.* Linen **napkin** by Liz Wain, $38, *at Bergdorf Goodman, 754 Fifth Avenue, New York, NY 10019; 212-753-7300.*

page 99

Baguette **coffee spoon**, $15, *at Dean & DeLuca, 560 Broadway, New York, NY 10012; 800-221-7714 or 212-431-1691.*

winter

page 106

Rimmed soup bowl, $50, *at Pierre Deux Antiques, 369 Bleecker Street, New York, NY 10014; 212-243-7740.*

page 107

Whiskey glass by Skruf's Glass Factory, $25, *at Lars Bolander Ltd., 5 Toilsome Lane, East Hampton, NY 11937; 516-329-3400.* Sterling-silver George III **dinner fork**, $100 each, *at I. Freeman & Son, 60 East 56th Street, New York, NY 10022; 212-759-6900.*

page 108

Bowl, $36, *at Simon Pearce, 500 Park Avenue at 59th Street, New York, NY 10022; 212-421-8801.* Georgian silver **serving fork**, $100, George III silver **tablespoon**, $140, *both at I. Freeman & Son, 60 East 56th Street, New York, NY 10022; 212-759-6900.* Linen **sheet**, $125, *at Susan Parrish, 390 Bleecker Street, New York, NY 10014; 212-645-5020.*

page 110

Linen **napkin** from a selection, $15 to $40, *from Frank McIntosh at Henri Bendel, 712 Fifth Avenue, New York, NY 10019; 212-247-1100.* French hotel silver-plate **flatware**, $110 for 5-piece place setting, *at Dean & DeLuca, 560 Broadway, New York, NY 10012; 800-221-7714 or 212-431-1691.*

page 112

Creil **platter**, $150, *at Pierre Deux Antiques, 369 Bleecker Street, New York, NY 10014; 212-243-7740.* Sage-green **napkin**, $20, *at Takashimaya, 693 Fifth Avenue, New York, NY 10022; 800-753-2038.*

page 113

Silver-marbled **bowl**, $95, **water glasses**, $20 each, blond-wood-handled **flatware**, $195 for 5-piece set, aqua-and-silver **dinner plate**, $50, *all at Takashimaya, 693 Fifth*

Avenue, New York, NY 10022; 800-753-2038.

page 115

Small oval celadon **serving platter,** $35, *at Simon Pearce, 500 Park Avenue at 59th Street, New York, NY 10022; 212-421-8801.*

page 116

Turkey sausage, $48.95 for 6 pounds, **chicken-apple sausage,** $37.95 for five 4-link packs, **pork sausage,** $48.95 for 6 pounds, *all available from Aidells Sausage Co., 1575 Minnesota Street, San Francisco, CA 94107; 415-285-6660 or 800-546-5795. Free catalogue. Other varieties available.*

page 117

Woodbine gold cotton-linen **napkin,** $31, *from Anichini. Call 800-553-5309 for nearest store locations.* George III **serving spoon,** $300 per pair, *at I. Freeman & Son, 60 East 56th Street, New York, NY 10022; 212-759-6900.*

page 118

Classico fringed linen-cotton **throw,** $138, Fonda Arpa fringed linen-cotton **napkin,** $31, *both from Anichini. Call 800-553-5309 for nearest store locations.* George IV **silver fork,** $200 for pair, Tiffany Flemish **dinner knife,** $600 for set of 6, *both at I. Freeman & Son, 60 East 56th Street, New York, NY 10022; 212-759-6900.*

page 119

Antique linen hemstitched **napkin,** $240 for set of 6, *from Anichini. Call 800-553-5309 for nearest store locations.*

pages 122, 123

Woven paisley **table cover,** $325, hand-worked linen **napkins,** $10 each, *both at Trouvaille Française, New York, NY; 212-737-6015 (by appointment only).* 4" tinned steel **flan rings,** $2.75 each, *at Dean & DeLuca, 560 Broadway, New York, NY 10012; 800-221-7714 or 212-431-1691.*

page 124

Paris-porcelain **cake plate,** $12, *at Charterhouse Antiques, 115 Greenwich Avenue, New York, NY 10014; 212-243-4726.*

page 125

Decanter, $45, and Wedgwood **plates,** $140 each, *at Charterhouse Antiques, 115 Greenwich Avenue, New York, NY 10014; 212-243-4726.*

page 127

French **salad plate** with gold-leaf rim, $95, *at Takashimaya, 693 Fifth Avenue, New York, NY 10022; 800-753-2038.*

page 128

Venetian-glass **bowl,** part of 21-piece dessert set, $1,875, *at Malmaison Antiques, 253 East 74th Street, New York, NY 10021; 212-288-7569.*

page 129

Nineteenth-century Wedding Band **dinner plate and side plate,** part of 128-piece set, $5,000, Venetian-glass **wineglass,** part of 21-piece dessert set, $1,875, *all at Malmaison Antiques, 253 East 74th Street, New York, NY 10021; 212-288-7569.* Handmade sterling-silver reproduction Irish Rib **knife,** $130 each, and **dinner fork,** $265 each, *both at James Robinson, 480 Park Avenue, New York, NY 10022; 212-752-6166.* Amber **glass rinser,** $550 for 2, *at James II Galleries Ltd., 11 East 57th Street, 4th floor, New York, NY 10022; 212-355-7040.* Williamsburg **candles,** $8.50 each, *at Pure Mädderlake, 478 Broadway, New York, NY 10013; 212-941-7770.*

page 130

Drabware **shaped dish** by Wedgwood, $5,250 for partial dessert service, *at James II Galleries Ltd., 11 East 57th Street, 4th floor, New York, NY 10022; 212-355-7040.*

page 131

Venetian-style green-and-gold **glass plate,**

$300 each, Venetian-glass **wineglass,** part of 21-piece dessert set, $1,875, *both at Malmaison Antiques, 253 East 74th Street, New York, NY 10021; 212-288-7569.* Handmade sterling-silver reproduction Irish Rib **dessert fork,** $180 each, *at James Robinson, 480 Park Avenue, New York, NY 10022; 212-752-6166.*

page 132

Bowl, $20, and **platter,** $18, both by Homer Laughlin, *from Fritz's American Wonder at the Tomato Factory, 2 Somerset Street, Hopewell, NJ 08525; 609-466-9833.* Potpourri **serving bowl** by Wedgwood, $95. *Call 800-677-7860 for nearest retailer.*

page 134

Eighteenth-century Italian **chairs,** $4,500 per pair, *at Reymer-Jourdan Antiques, 43 East 10th Street, New York, NY 10003; 212-674-4470.* Patrician silverplate **flatware** by Community, $10 per piece, *from Country Cupboard at the Tomato Factory, 2 Somerset Street, Hopewell, NJ 08525; 609-466-9833.* Queensplain **dinner plates,** $11.90 each, and **butter plates,** $5.60 each, both by Wedgwood. *Call 800-677-7860 for retailers.* Platinum-blue **dinner plates** by Schammell, $10 each, *from Hopewell Antique Center at the Tomato Factory, 2 Somerset Street, Hopewell, NJ 08525; 609-466-2990.* **Polka-dot glasses** by Fenton, $30 each, and **clear blue pressed-glass goblets,** $60 for set of 8, *all at Fran Jay's Depression Glass, 10 Church Street, Lambertville, NJ 08530; 609-397-1571.* **Vase** (circa 1940) by Trenton Art China, $24, *from Sim at the Tomato Factory, 2 Somerset Street, Hopewell, NJ 08525; 609-466-9833.*

pages 134, 135

Linen **napkins,** $5 each, *from Sim at the Tomato Factory, 2 Somerset Street, Hopewell, NJ 08525; 609-466-9833.*

index

credits